Consulting 102:

Part 2
Communication and Interpersonal Skills

Preface

I'm glad to see you again! It's been a little while since we haven't talked. But don't you worry, I remember exactly where we left off.

In this second volume of my Consulting 102 series, we'll focus on enhancing your communication and interpersonal skills. This book will cover advanced presentation and facilitation techniques, executive presence and influence, and emotional intelligence. By honing these skills, you will be able to effectively engage with clients, facilitate meaningful conversations, and build strong and lasting relationships.

My aim is always the same: to empower you with the skills, knowledge, and mindset to excel in the consulting profession. So, buckle up and get ready for an enriching and transformative journey!

As with my previous books on consulting, one of my main goals with this new Consulting 102 series is to present the material in a clear and accessible manner. I understand that the consulting world can be filled with jargon and complex terminology, so I've made it a priority to communicate these concepts in a relatable and easy-to-understand way. I hope that I've achieved this goal and that you find the content approachable and engaging.

In addition to clarity, practicality is also at the forefront of this series. Throughout the chapters, you'll find practical examples and exercises that will help you apply the concepts and techniques in real-world scenarios. By providing you with tangible tools and resources, I aim to bridge the gap between theory and practice, allowing you to immediately start implementing what you learn.

It's important to remember that consulting is a continuous learning journey. As you navigate through this guide, I encourage you to embrace curiosity, challenge yourself, and adopt a growth mindset. The advanced skills and knowledge you will acquire here will empower you to overcome complex challenges, make a meaningful impact, and become a trusted advisor to your clients.

But let's not waste any more time and dive right into Part 2! I hope that you find this second module to be a valuable resource in your consulting journey.

Here's to your success as an advanced consultant!

Sincerely,

Cai Everdeen.

Introduction

Alright. Let's get going on Part 2 of *"Consulting 102: The Advanced Guide for Consultants"* – Advanced Communication and Interpersonal Skills! In this second volume, we will delve into the art of effective communication, understanding human dynamics, and building strong relationships with clients and stakeholders. Get ready to sharpen your communication prowess and master the skills necessary to excel in the world of consulting.

Chapter 9, *"Advanced Presentation Skills,"* is all about taking your presentation abilities to the next level. Learn how to captivate your audience, craft compelling narratives, and deliver impactful presentations that leave a lasting impression.

In Chapter 10, *"Advanced Facilitation Skills,"* we explore the art of guiding group discussions and workshops. Discover how to create engaging and productive sessions, facilitate collaboration, and elicit meaningful insights from diverse perspectives.

Chapter 11, *"Executive Presence and Influence,"* delves into the qualities and behaviors that exude confidence and command respect. Unlock the secrets of executive presence, learn how to effectively influence key decision-makers, and navigate complex power dynamics.

Prepare to harness the power of storytelling in Chapter 12, *"Storytelling for Consulting."* Discover how to leverage the persuasive power of narratives to convey complex ideas, connect with your audience on an emotional level, and drive meaningful change.

In Chapter 13, *"Advanced Negotiation Skills,"* we dive into the art of negotiation. Explore advanced techniques, strategies, and tactics to achieve win-win outcomes, build collaborative relationships, and successfully navigate complex negotiations.

Chapter 14, *"Emotional Intelligence for Consulting,"* focuses on understanding and managing emotions, both yours and those of others. Develop your emotional intelligence to build rapport, navigate challenging situations, and foster effective working relationships.

In Chapter 15, *"Conflict Resolution and Management,"* we tackle the challenges of dealing with conflict in a professional setting. Learn effective strategies for resolving conflicts, promoting healthy dialogue, and building consensus among stakeholders.

Chapter 16, *"Cross-Cultural Communication,"* takes you on a journey of understanding and embracing cultural diversity. Gain insights into different cultural norms, communication styles, and practices, enabling you to navigate cross-cultural interactions with finesse.

Throughout this second volume, as always, I will share amusing and relatable anecdotes that highlight the importance and practical applications of these communication and interpersonal skills. So, get ready to enhance your consulting prowess, connect with others authentically, and build strong relationships that drive success. Let's embark on this enlightening journey together and unlock the advanced communication and interpersonal skills that will set you apart as a consultant.

Table of Content

CHAPTER 14: EMOTIONAL INTELLIGENCE FOR CONSULTING -------181

Chapter 9: Advanced Presentation Skills

I hope you're ready to take your presentation skills to the next level because we're about to dive into the world of advanced presentations. Picture this: You're standing in front of a room full of executives, all eagerly awaiting your insights and recommendations. As you begin your presentation, you notice how their eyes light up, their attention focused solely on you. You feel confident, knowing that you have their undivided attention and that your message is resonating with them. This is the power of advanced presentation skills, and I'm excited to guide you on this journey.

But before we jump into the nitty-gritty details of advanced presentations, let me take a moment to introduce myself. I'm Cai Everdeen, and I've been in the consulting world for quite some time now. Over the years, I've had my fair share of highs and lows when it comes to presentations. I've experienced moments of triumph when my presentations have wowed clients and left a lasting impact. And I've also had my fair share of challenges and lessons learned along the way.

You see, presentations are not just about delivering information. They're about connecting with your audience, inspiring action, and making a memorable impression. And that's exactly what we'll be exploring in this chapter – the advanced techniques and strategies that will help you become a master presenter.

Throughout this chapter, we'll delve into various aspects of advanced presentations. We'll discuss how to craft compelling narratives, capture attention from the very first slide, and use visual aids to enhance your message. We'll also explore techniques for managing nerves and building rapport with your audience. In addition, we'll dive into the world of storytelling, leveraging emotions, and mastering the art of persuasion.

But don't worry, I won't just be sharing theoretical concepts with you. Along the way, I'll be sharing personal anecdotes and experiences from my own consulting journey, which seems like a never-ending journey of learning and awe moments. I'll give you practical tips and actionable advice that you can implement right away to elevate your presentation skills.

So, if you're ready to captivate your audience, leave a lasting impression, and become a true master of the presentation craft, then let's dive into the world of advanced presentation skills. Together, we'll unlock the secrets to delivering presentations that will leave your clients in awe and set you apart as an exceptional consultant.

Get ready to shine on that stage, my friends. The spotlight is waiting for you!

Introduction to Advanced Presentation Skills

As I stand here, about to deliver a presentation to a room full of influential executives, I can't help but feel a mix of nerves and excitement. This is a crucial moment, where I have the opportunity to impress and influence these decision-makers. Over the years, I have honed my presentation skills to a point where I can confidently say that I have mastered the art of delivering impactful presentations. In this chapter, I will guide you through the world of advanced presentation skills, where we will explore the fundamental principles and concepts that will elevate your ability to captivate and engage your audience.

Advanced Presentation Skills refers to the ability to deliver highly effective and impactful presentations that captivate and engage the audience. It goes beyond the basics of public speaking and encompasses a range of advanced techniques and strategies to deliver presentations that leave a lasting impression. Advanced presentation skills involve not only the delivery of information but also the ability to connect with the audience, tell compelling stories, use visual aids effectively, manage nerves, and persuade and influence others. These skills are essential for consultants who need to convey complex ideas, influence stakeholders, and make persuasive recommendations to clients.

Key Concepts, Techniques, and Tools

I'm excited to delve into this topic with you because, let's face it, delivering a powerful presentation can make all the difference in a consulting engagement. Picture this: you're standing in front of a room filled with influential stakeholders, ready to present your findings and recommendations. The success of your presentation can determine the fate of the project and your credibility as a consultant. It's a pivotal moment, and that's where advanced presentation skills come into play.

But before we jump into the nitty-gritty of techniques and tools, let's explore the fundamental principles and concepts that underpin advanced presentation skills. Understanding these core ideas will lay the foundation for your journey towards becoming a master presenter.

Concept 1: Understanding Your Audience

First and foremost, we'll focus on the concept of understanding your audience. One of the key concepts in advanced presentation skills is indeed understanding your audience. This involves conducting thorough research to gain insights into their needs, interests, and preferences. By understanding your audience, you can tailor your message and delivery to resonate with them effectively. It's crucial to recognize that every audience is unique, with their own needs, interests, and preferences. By conducting thorough research and analysis, you can gain valuable insights into your audience's expectations and tailor your presentation to address their specific concerns. Remember, a one-size-fits-all approach won't cut it when it comes to advanced presentations.

Understanding Your Audience refers to the ability to gather insights and knowledge about the individuals or group you will be presenting to. As a consultant, getting the most out of this understanding is essential for delivering a successful presentation.

To effectively understand your audience, start by conducting thorough research and analysis. Dive into their background, industry, and specific roles within the organization. This will help you tailor your message and presentation style to resonate with their interests and concerns. Consider their level of expertise and familiarity with the subject matter to determine the appropriate level of detail to include.

Engage in conversations and interviews with key stakeholders prior to the presentation to gain valuable insights into their expectations, challenges, and desired outcomes. This will allow you to align your presentation with their needs and address any potential objections or doubts they may have.

Another valuable strategy is to consider the cultural and organizational context in which your audience operates. Different cultures and organizations may have unique communication styles, expectations, and preferences. Adjust your presentation approach accordingly to ensure maximum impact and engagement.

During the presentation, actively observe your audience's reactions, body language, and level of engagement. Pay attention to cues such as nodding, facial expressions, and note-taking. This will help you gauge their level of understanding and adjust your pace, tone, or level of detail as needed.

To get the most out of understanding your audience as a consultant, always strive for empathy and adaptability. Put yourself in their shoes and tailor your presentation to address their specific needs and interests. By doing so, you will build credibility, establish rapport, and increase the likelihood of your message resonating with the audience.

Remember, a successful presentation is not just about delivering information, but also about connecting with your audience on an emotional level and inspiring them to take action. By understanding your audience deeply, you can craft a presentation that speaks directly to their concerns and motivates them to embrace your ideas and recommendations.

Concept 2: Compelling Message and Structure

Next, we'll dive into the importance of creating a compelling message and structure. Creating a compelling message and structuring your presentation is essential for capturing and maintaining your audience's attention. This includes defining a clear objective, developing a storyline, and organizing your content in a logical and engaging manner. Techniques such as the storytelling framework can help you connect with your audience on an emotional level.

You want your presentation to be more than just a collection of slides or talking points. It should have a clear objective and a well-defined storyline that captivates your audience from start to finish. We'll explore techniques like storytelling, where you can weave a narrative that engages emotions and connects with your audience on a deeper level. A compelling message and a well-structured presentation are essential for delivering your ideas effectively.

A compelling message and structure are essential components of an impactful presentation. They ensure that your audience is engaged, your ideas are effectively communicated, and your presentation leaves a lasting impression. As a consultant, crafting a compelling message and structure involves the following key elements:

Clarity of Objective: Clearly define the purpose of your presentation. What do you want to achieve? Whether it's to inform, persuade, or inspire, having a clear objective will guide your content and help you stay focused throughout.

Storytelling: Weave a narrative that captures your audience's attention and resonates with them on an emotional level. Tell a story that illustrates your key points, incorporates real-world examples, or shares relevant anecdotes. This storytelling approach humanizes your presentation and makes it more relatable and memorable. We'll dive further into what storytelling is all about in a subsequent chapter.

Logical Flow: Structure your presentation in a logical and coherent manner. Start with an engaging introduction that grabs attention and sets the context. Organize your main points or ideas into a logical sequence, ensuring a smooth transition between each section. Conclude your presentation with a strong and memorable closing that reinforces your key message.

Visual Hierarchy: Use visual aids, such as slides, to support your message and enhance understanding. Ensure that your visuals are visually appealing, easy to read, and convey information effectively. Use a consistent visual hierarchy to guide your audience's attention and emphasize key points.

Conciseness and Relevance: Keep your content concise and focused. Avoid overwhelming your audience with too much information. Instead, prioritize the most relevant and impactful points. Be mindful of your audience's time and attention span, delivering a presentation that is concise and to the point.

To get the most out of a compelling message and structure as a consultant, consider the following tips:

Know Your Audience: Tailor your message and structure to the specific needs, interests, and preferences of your audience. Understand their background, expectations, and knowledge level. This understanding will allow you to customize your content and delivery to resonate with your audience.

Align with Client Objectives: Ensure that your message aligns with the objectives of your client or the project you're working on. Demonstrate how your presentation adds value and contributes to their goals. By aligning your message with their objectives, you can establish credibility and gain their support.

Practice and Refine: Practice your presentation multiple times to refine your message and structure. Pay attention to your delivery, timing, and transitions between sections. Seek feedback from trusted colleagues or mentors to identify areas for improvement and make necessary adjustments.

Engage and Connect: Engage your audience throughout the presentation by using interactive elements, asking thought-provoking questions, or incorporating group activities. Connect with your audience by maintaining eye contact, using expressive body language, and speaking with enthusiasm and passion.

By incorporating these principles and techniques into your presentations, you can ensure that your message is compelling, your structure is effective, and your audience is captivated. A compelling message and structure will enhance your ability to communicate your ideas, gain buy-in from stakeholders, and make a lasting impact as a consultant.

Concept 3: Visual Aids

Visual aids are another key component of advanced presentation skills. Visual aids such as slides, videos, and infographics can enhance your presentation by visually representing key points and supporting your message. Effective use of visual aids involves keeping them simple, relevant, and visually appealing. Tools like PowerPoint, Keynote, or Prezi can help you create visually impactful presentations. And so, in this section, we'll discuss how to leverage tools like PowerPoint, Keynote, or Prezi to create visually appealing and impactful presentations. Remember, the goal is not to overwhelm your audience with a barrage of text and graphics but to use visuals strategically to support your message and enhance understanding.

Visual aids refer to the use of visual elements, such as slides, charts, graphs, images, and diagrams, to support and enhance presentations. As a consultant, leveraging visual aids effectively can significantly enhance your communication and make your message more engaging and memorable. Here are some tips to get the most out of visual aids:

Keep it simple and focused: Visual aids should be clear, concise, and easy to understand. Avoid cluttering your slides with excessive text or complex graphics. Use visuals that directly support your key points and help your audience grasp the information quickly.

Use visuals strategically: Visual aids should serve as a complement to your presentation, not as a substitute for your verbal communication. Use visuals to illustrate data, highlight key concepts, or emphasize important points. Remember to use relevant and high-quality visuals that align with your message and resonate with your audience.

Maintain consistency: Create a consistent visual theme throughout your presentation. Use a cohesive color scheme, font style, and formatting to ensure a professional and polished look. Consistency in design helps to establish credibility and make your presentation visually appealing.

Practice proper timing: Control the timing of your visual aids to maintain a smooth flow of your presentation. Avoid overwhelming your audience with too many visuals or leaving them on the screen for too long. Time your visuals to appear at the right moment to reinforce your message effectively.

Explain and interpret visuals: Don't assume that your audience will understand the meaning of your visuals without explanation. Take the time to explain and interpret the visuals to ensure clarity and understanding. Provide context and insights that help your audience connect the visual information with your main points.

Engage with your audience: Visual aids can be a powerful tool to engage your audience. Use visuals to facilitate discussions, ask questions, or encourage participation. Incorporate interactive elements, such as polls or interactive diagrams, to involve your audience actively.

Prepare backup options: Technical glitches can happen, so be prepared with backup options. Have printed handouts or alternative presentation formats ready in case of technical difficulties. This ensures that your message can still be effectively delivered, even if there are unforeseen issues.

By leveraging visual aids effectively, you can enhance your presentations, make complex information more digestible, and leave a lasting impression on your clients and stakeholders. Visual aids can help you communicate your ideas more persuasively and engage your audience on a deeper level.

Tool 1: PowerPoint

PowerPoint is a widely used software tool for creating visual aids and presentations. It allows users to design and organize content in a structured and visually appealing manner. When it comes to advanced presentation skills and creating effective visual aids, PowerPoint can be a valuable tool. Here are some key aspects to consider:

Structure and Organization: PowerPoint helps you structure your presentation by providing slides that act as individual components of your overall message. Use the slide layout options to create a clear and logical flow. Start with a strong introduction, outline your main points, and conclude with a memorable closing. Each slide should have a clear purpose and contribute to the overall message.

Visual Design: PowerPoint enables you to create visually engaging slides. Use consistent color schemes, fonts, and layouts to maintain a professional and cohesive look. Incorporate relevant images, charts, graphs, and icons to visually represent your ideas and make them more memorable. Avoid cluttered slides and aim for simplicity and clarity in your design.

Content Enhancement: PowerPoint allows you to enhance your content through the use of bullet points, headings, and subheadings. Keep your text concise and use keywords or phrases to highlight key messages. Utilize features like animations, transitions, and multimedia elements sparingly to add interest and engagement, but avoid overusing them, as they can distract from your message.

Audience Engagement: PowerPoint offers features that can help engage your audience during the presentation. Use slide animations to reveal information gradually and build anticipation. Incorporate interactive elements like polls, quizzes, or discussion prompts to encourage audience participation. Additionally, use speaker notes or presenter view to guide your presentation and ensure a smooth delivery.

Visual Data Representation: PowerPoint allows you to present data effectively through charts, graphs, and tables. Use appropriate chart types to represent your data accurately and in a visually appealing way. Ensure that the data is easy to read and understand, and provide clear labels and titles. Use visual cues, such as colors and patterns, to differentiate data points and highlight key insights.

When using PowerPoint for advanced presentation skills and creating visual aids, remember that it is a tool to support your message, not the focal point of your presentation. Use it strategically to enhance your content and engage your audience, but always prioritize clear communication and effective delivery.

Tool 2: Keynote

Keynotes are a popular software application developed by Apple Inc. It is primarily used for creating and delivering presentations. When it comes to advanced presentation skills and creating visual aids, Keynote offers several features and benefits:

Professional Design: Keynote provides a wide range of professionally designed templates, themes, and layouts that can enhance the visual appeal of your presentations. These templates can be customized to match your branding or specific needs, making it easier to create visually stunning slides.

Multimedia Integration: Keynote allows you to easily incorporate multimedia elements such as images, videos, audio, and animations into your presentations. This enables you to create dynamic and engaging visual aids that capture and maintain audience attention.

Animation and Transition Effects: Keynote offers a variety of animation and transition effects that can be applied to individual slides or objects within the slides. These effects can help you effectively communicate your message, highlight key points, and create visual interest.

Collaboration and Sharing: Keynote allows for easy collaboration with team members or clients. Multiple people can work on the same presentation simultaneously, and changes can be tracked and synchronized in real-time. Additionally, Keynote presentations can be easily shared with others via email, cloud storage platforms, or through web links.

Presenter Tools: Keynote provides useful presenter tools to enhance your delivery during presentations. This includes features like presenter notes, timer, and slide navigation, which can help you stay organized and deliver a smooth and engaging presentation.

Export and Compatibility: Keynote presentations can be exported to various formats such as PDF, PowerPoint, and QuickTime movie. This ensures compatibility and enables seamless sharing with individuals who may not have access to Keynote.

When using Keynote for advanced presentation skills, it is important to focus on creating visually appealing slides that support and enhance your message. Avoid overloading slides with excessive text or cluttered visuals. Instead, use concise and impactful content, complemented by appropriate images, charts, and graphs. Practice your delivery to ensure a confident and engaging presentation that effectively communicates your ideas and engages the audience.

Tool 3: Prezi

Prezi is a cloud-based presentation software that allows users to create dynamic and visually appealing presentations. It offers a unique approach to storytelling and presentation design, making it a popular tool for advanced presentation skills and creating engaging visual aids.

Key features and benefits of Prezi include:

Non-linear storytelling: Unlike traditional slide-based presentations, Prezi allows you to create a canvas where you can zoom in and out, pan across, and create paths between different points of information. This non-linear approach enables you to create more interactive and engaging presentations that can hold the audience's attention.

Visual appeal: Prezi offers a wide range of customizable templates, themes, and layouts to create visually stunning presentations. You can incorporate images, videos, charts, and other multimedia elements to enhance your message and create a memorable visual experience.

Collaboration: Prezi allows multiple users to collaborate on a presentation in real-time. This feature is particularly useful for teams working on consulting projects together, as it enables seamless collaboration and feedback sharing.

Data visualization: Prezi offers various data visualization tools, such as charts, graphs, and infographics, that can help you present complex information in a visually engaging and easy-to-understand manner. This is especially useful when presenting data-heavy insights or analysis to clients.

Audience engagement: Prezi's dynamic presentation style helps keep the audience engaged throughout the presentation. By utilizing features like zooming and panning, you can create a sense of motion and interactivity, making the presentation more memorable and impactful.

When using Prezi for advanced presentation skills and creating visual aids, it's important to keep a few things in mind:

Focus on storytelling: Prezi's unique features allow you to create a narrative flow in your presentation. Use this opportunity to craft a compelling story that connects with your audience and effectively communicates your message.

Keep it concise: Avoid overcrowding your presentation with too much text or visuals. Use Prezi's zooming and panning features strategically to guide the audience's attention and emphasize key points.

Practice and rehearse: While Prezi offers a dynamic and visually engaging platform, it's essential to practice and rehearse your presentation to ensure a smooth delivery. Pay attention to your timing, transitions, and overall flow of the presentation.

Overall, Prezi can be a valuable tool for consultants looking to enhance their presentation skills and create impactful visual aids. By leveraging its unique features and focusing on effective storytelling, you can create engaging and memorable presentations that leave a lasting impression on your audience.

And on that note, let's move on; let us be persuasive!

Concept 4: Persuasive Communication

Persuasive communication techniques can help you influence and engage your audience. This includes using rhetorical devices, such as storytelling, metaphors, and analogies, to convey your message effectively. Techniques like the power of three and the rule of reciprocity can enhance the persuasiveness of your presentation.

Persuasive communication is the art of influencing others and convincing them to adopt a particular viewpoint, take specific actions, or make decisions in line with your recommendations. As a consultant, mastering persuasive communication is essential for effectively engaging with clients, building trust, and driving positive outcomes. Here are some strategies to get the most out of persuasive communication as a consultant:

Understand your audience: Tailor your message to resonate with your audience's needs, interests, and values. Conduct thorough research to identify their motivations and concerns, and craft your communication to address those directly.

Build credibility: Establish yourself as a credible and knowledgeable expert in your field. Demonstrate your expertise through case studies, success stories, and data-driven insights. When your audience sees you as a trusted advisor, they will be more likely to be influenced by your message.

Craft a compelling message: Develop a clear and concise message that highlights the benefits and value of your recommendations. Structure your message in a way that captures attention, engages emotions, and presents a logical flow of ideas. Use storytelling techniques to create a narrative that connects with your audience on an emotional level.

Use persuasive language: Choose your words carefully to evoke emotions, create a sense of urgency, and inspire action. Employ rhetorical devices such as metaphors, analogies, and powerful imagery to make your message more memorable and persuasive.

Support your arguments with evidence: Back up your recommendations with relevant data, facts, and examples. Use credible sources and statistics to strengthen your arguments and increase your persuasiveness.

Adapt your communication style: Be mindful of your audience's communication preferences and adapt your style accordingly. Some may respond better to a more formal and structured approach, while others may prefer a conversational and informal tone. Flexibility in your communication style allows you to connect with different individuals and engage them more effectively.

Listen actively: Effective persuasion involves listening to your audience's concerns, objections, and feedback. Actively listen to their perspectives, ask clarifying questions, and demonstrate empathy. By understanding their viewpoint, you can address their concerns and tailor your message accordingly.

Anticipate and address objections: Identify potential objections or barriers that may prevent your audience from accepting your recommendations. Anticipate these objections and address them proactively in your communication. Offer compelling arguments, alternative solutions, or evidence to counter their concerns.

Practice and refine your delivery: Delivering a persuasive message requires practice and refinement. Rehearse your presentation, pay attention to your body language, vocal tone, and overall delivery. Seek feedback from trusted colleagues or mentors to improve your persuasive communication skills.

By incorporating these strategies into your consulting practice, you can enhance your ability to persuade and influence others effectively.

Concept 5: Body Language and Vocal Techniques

Your body language and vocal techniques play a significant role in delivering an impactful presentation. Nonverbal communication plays a significant role in delivering an impactful presentation. Body language, including gestures, facial expressions, and posture, can help convey confidence and engage your audience. Vocal techniques, such as tone, pace, and emphasis, can add emphasis and convey your message with clarity and impact. And so, let us dive into the art of nonverbal communication, including gestures, facial expressions, and posture.

Body language and vocal techniques are essential components of effective communication in presentations. As a consultant, leveraging these skills can greatly enhance your ability to connect with your audience and convey your message persuasively. Here's how you can get the most out of body language and vocal techniques:

Body Language: Your body language includes gestures, facial expressions, posture, and movement. To make the most of your body language as a consultant:

- Use open and confident body postures. Stand tall, with your shoulders back, and maintain an open stance to appear approachable and confident.
- Use purposeful and natural gestures to emphasize key points. Avoid excessive or distracting movements that may detract from your message.
- Maintain eye contact with your audience. It shows that you are engaged and interested in their response.

- Mirror the body language of your audience to establish rapport and connection.

Vocal Techniques: Your voice is a powerful tool in conveying your message effectively. To maximize your vocal impact:

- Use a confident and clear voice. Speak with authority and conviction to inspire confidence in your audience.
- Vary your tone, pitch, and pace to create interest and emphasize important points. A monotone voice can be dull and disengage your audience.
- Use pauses strategically. Pauses can help to create emphasis, allow the audience to absorb information, and add dramatic effect to your delivery.
- Practice proper articulation and enunciation to ensure that your words are clear and easily understood.

To get the most out of body language and vocal techniques, it's important to practice and observe yourself. Record your presentations and review them to identify areas for improvement. Seek feedback from trusted colleagues or mentors who can provide constructive criticism. Additionally, consider attending workshops or courses on public speaking or communication skills to further enhance your abilities. Remember, mastering body language and vocal techniques takes time and practice. By incorporating these skills into your presentations, you can engage your audience, convey confidence, and make a lasting impact as a consultant.

Concept 6: Q&A and Handling Difficult Questions

Being prepared to handle questions and engage in Q&A sessions is crucial for advanced presentation skills. Techniques such as active listening, paraphrasing, and providing concise and confident responses can help you navigate challenging questions and maintain control of the presentation. Advanced presenters are adept at handling difficult questions with grace and confidence. We'll discuss techniques such as active listening, paraphrasing, and providing concise and confident responses that address the question effectively.

Q&A (Questions and Answers) sessions are an integral part of presentations and consultations. This is the time when the audience has the opportunity to seek clarification, challenge your ideas, and engage in a meaningful dialogue with you. Handling difficult questions during Q&A requires finesse and confidence.

Here's how you can get the most out of it as a consultant:

Prepare in advance: Anticipate potential questions that may arise based on your presentation content. Consider the perspectives and concerns of your audience. Prepare thoughtful and well-reasoned responses to address these questions.

Active listening: During the Q&A session, actively listen to the question being asked. Pay attention to the nuances and the underlying concerns. By fully understanding the question, you can provide a more relevant and targeted response.

Pause and reflect: Take a moment before responding to difficult questions. This pause allows you to gather your thoughts, maintain composure, and respond with clarity. It's okay to acknowledge that a question is challenging and that you need a moment to provide a thoughtful response.

Stay composed and confident: Even if a question catches you off guard or challenges your expertise, it's important to remain composed and confident. Maintain good eye contact, use assertive body language, and speak with conviction. Your confidence will instill trust and credibility in your audience.

Paraphrase and clarify: When faced with complex or unclear questions, paraphrase the question to ensure you understand it correctly. This not only shows respect to the questioner but also gives you the opportunity to seek clarification if needed. Clarifying the question will enable you to provide a more targeted and accurate response.

Provide concise and relevant answers: Keep your responses concise and focused. Avoid going off on tangents or providing excessive information. Address the core of the question and provide a clear and direct answer. If the question requires a more detailed response, offer to follow up after the session.

Stay professional and respectful: It's important to maintain professionalism and respect, even when faced with challenging or confrontational questions. Avoid becoming defensive or engaging in arguments. Respond in a calm and composed manner, focusing on the facts and maintaining a respectful tone.

Learn from each interaction: Treat each Q&A session as an opportunity for growth and learning. Reflect on the questions asked and the responses provided. Consider how you can improve your communication, address gaps in knowledge, and enhance your presentation in future engagements.

By mastering the art of Q&A and handling difficult questions, you can showcase your expertise, build trust with your audience, and demonstrate your ability to handle challenging situations. Embrace these moments as opportunities for growth and refinement, and you'll excel as a consultant.

Concept 7: Practice and Rehearsal

Lastly, we'll emphasize the importance of practice and rehearsal. Regular practice and rehearsal are essential for honing your presentation skills. Like any skill, advanced presentation skills require regular practice to refine your delivery, timing, and overall performance. This includes practicing your delivery, refining your timing, and ensuring a smooth flow of your presentation. Rehearsing in front of a mirror, recording yourself, or seeking feedback from peers can help you identify areas for improvement and enhance your overall performance.

Practice and rehearsal are essential components of advanced presentation skills. They involve repeatedly going over your presentation, refining your delivery, and familiarizing yourself with the content. When done effectively, practice and rehearsal can significantly enhance your confidence, clarity, and overall performance as a consultant. Here are some key tips to get the most out of your practice and rehearsal sessions:

Start early: Begin practicing well in advance of your presentation to allow ample time for improvement. Procrastination can lead to rushed preparation and increased anxiety.

Break it down: Divide your presentation into manageable sections or key points. Practice each section separately before integrating them into a cohesive presentation. This approach helps ensure that you thoroughly understand and master each element.

Focus on delivery: Pay attention to your body language, vocal tone, and pacing. Practice using gestures, maintaining eye contact, and varying your voice to engage your audience and convey your message effectively.

Use visuals sparingly: If you're using visual aids like slides, practice incorporating them seamlessly into your presentation. Ensure they enhance your message without overshadowing your delivery or becoming a crutch.

Seek feedback: Invite trusted colleagues, mentors, or friends to provide constructive feedback on your presentation. They can offer valuable insights and help identify areas for improvement.

Record yourself: Use a video or audio recording device to capture your practice sessions. Review the recordings to assess your strengths and areas that need refinement. This allows you to objectively evaluate your performance and make necessary adjustments.

Time management: Practice your presentation within the allotted time frame. Pay attention to your pacing and ensure you can deliver your content concisely without rushing or exceeding the time limit.

Rehearse in different settings: Practice in various environments, such as a quiet room, a simulated meeting space, or even in front of a small audience if possible. This helps you adapt to different settings and prepares you for unexpected challenges.

Embrace feedback and make adjustments: Be open to receiving feedback and be willing to make adjustments based on the suggestions you receive. Remember, practice is all about refining your skills and continuously improving your presentation.

Visualize success: Use visualization techniques to imagine yourself delivering a successful presentation. Visualize yourself confidently engaging your audience, receiving positive feedback, and achieving your desired outcomes. This mental rehearsal can boost your confidence and performance.

By dedicating time and effort to practice and rehearsal, you can enhance your presentation skills, boost your confidence, and deliver impactful presentations as a consultant. Remember, practice makes progress, and the more you invest in honing your skills, the more successful and influential you will become as a presenter.

Tools 4: Technology and Presentation Tools

Utilizing technology and presentation tools effectively can enhance your presentation. This may include using interactive features, incorporating multimedia elements, or utilizing online platforms for virtual presentations. Familiarizing yourself with presentation software, collaboration tools, and virtual meeting platforms can enhance your presentation delivery. Technology and Presentation Tools are indeed essential elements of advanced presentation skills. In today's digital age, consultants have access to a wide range of technological tools that can enhance the effectiveness and impact of their presentations. These tools can help create visually appealing slides, incorporate multimedia elements, and facilitate interactive experiences with the audience.

To get the most out of technology and presentation tools as a consultant, it's important to consider a few key points. First, familiarize yourself with the available tools and choose the ones that best align with your presentation style and objectives. Common presentation tools include Microsoft PowerPoint, Google Slides, Keynote, and Prezi, among others. Explore their features, experiment with different templates and layouts, and become proficient in using them.

When using technology and presentation tools, keep in mind the principle of simplicity. While these tools offer a myriad of options, it's crucial to avoid overwhelming your audience with excessive animations, transitions, or complex designs. Strive for clarity and focus on delivering your message effectively. Use visuals, graphs, and diagrams to illustrate key points and make complex information easier to understand.

Another aspect to consider is the integration of multimedia elements. Technology allows you to incorporate videos, audio clips, and interactive content into your presentations. Utilize these elements strategically to engage and captivate your audience. However, ensure that the multimedia elements align with your message and enhance the overall presentation rather than distract from it.

Furthermore, consider the logistics of using technology during your presentation. Test the equipment and software in advance to avoid technical glitches. Have backup plans in case of any unforeseen issues. Familiarize yourself with the venue's setup and any necessary adapters or connectors you may need. Being prepared and confident in using the technology will help you deliver a seamless and professional presentation.

Lastly, remember that technology and presentation tools are means to an end. While they can enhance your presentation, they should not overshadow the content and your delivery. Focus on crafting a compelling message, engaging with your audience, and delivering your presentation with confidence. The technology should serve as a tool to support your message and create an impactful experience for your audience.

By leveraging technology and presentation tools effectively, you can elevate your presentations to a new level, engage your audience, and leave a lasting impression as a consultant. Embrace the possibilities that technology offers, experiment with different features, and continuously seek ways to enhance your presentation skills in the digital age.

Practical Examples

Let me share a couple of practical examples to illustrate how advanced presentation skills can benefit a consultant in real-life scenarios.

Example 1: Complex Data Analysis Presentation

I was once tasked with presenting the findings of a complex data analysis to a client's executive team. I knew that simply presenting a barrage of numbers and charts won't effectively communicate the insights and recommendations. Instead, I did my best to create a compelling narrative. Using storytelling techniques, I crafted a storyline that connected the data points to the client's strategic objectives. I then incorporated visually appealing infographics and interactive visualizations to make the data more accessible and engaging for the audience. The presentation also included real-life case studies and success stories to provide concrete examples of how the recommendations have worked for other clients. By applying advanced presentation skills, I was able to captivate the executive team, effectively communicate the insights, and secure buy-in for the proposed strategies.

Example 2: Process Improvement Initiative

In another scenario, I was presenting a proposal for a new process improvement initiative to a cross-functional team. I knew that the success of the proposal relied not only on the content but also on engaging and inspiring the team. And so, I created a visually impactful slide deck that highlighted the current pain points and the benefits of the proposed changes. I incorporated storytelling techniques to convey the impact of the initiative on individual team members, departments, and the organization as a whole. To facilitate interaction, I did a few live polls and Q&A sessions throughout the presentation, encouraging active participation and gathering feedback. By these simple but impactful techniques, I was able to create a persuasive and dynamic presentation that fostered collaboration, enthusiasm, and commitment from the team members. Granted, at the end of the presentation, the client executives didn't sign the proposal, but they did come back a year later, asking for assistance...

I hope these two examples highlight how advanced presentation skills go beyond simply delivering information. They involve strategic storytelling, visual design, interactive elements, and audience engagement techniques. By mastering these skills, you can effectively convey their message, build credibility, and inspire action among their audience.

Challenges and Common Mistakes to Avoid

As I stand before a room full of eager faces, I can't help but feel a sense of excitement and a touch of nervousness. The presentation I am about to deliver is crucial, and I want to make sure it leaves a lasting impact on my audience.

Over the years, I have learned some valuable lessons about advanced presentation skills - the challenges to overcome and the mistakes to avoid. In this chapter, I will share those insights with you, my fellow consultants, as we embark on a journey to master the art of advanced presentations. When it comes to applying advanced presentation skills, there are several common challenges and mistakes that consultants should be aware of and strive to avoid.

Some of these include:

Challenge 1: Overloading the presentation with information

Imagine this - you're presenting a complex idea to your clients, and you want to impress them with your expertise. The temptation to include every detail can be overwhelming. However, I've learned that less is often more when it comes to presentations. By focusing on the key messages and keeping the content concise and clear, you can avoid overwhelming your audience and ensure that your main points shine through. One common mistake is trying to include too much information in a presentation, leading to overwhelming the audience. It's important to focus on the key messages and keep the content concise and clear.

Challenge 2: Lack of audience focus

As consultants, our presentations should always revolve around our audience's needs and interests. Picture yourself in front of a diverse group of stakeholders, each with different priorities and expectations. Understanding your audience is crucial to delivering a presentation that resonates with them. Take the time to research and gather insights about your audience so that you can tailor your message accordingly and create a meaningful connection.

Challenge 3: Poor slide design

We've all been there - sitting through a presentation with cluttered, text-heavy slides that are more confusing than enlightening. Effective slide design is an art that can make or break a presentation. I've found that using clear and legible fonts, incorporating relevant graphics and images, and maintaining a consistent design theme can greatly enhance the impact of your message. Remember, your slides should support and enhance your presentation, not distract from it.

Challenge 4: Lack of storytelling and structure

Stories have a magical ability to captivate and engage an audience. As consultants, we should harness this power in our presentations. Think about a time when you were hooked by a story that unfolded during a presentation. By incorporating storytelling techniques, you can create a compelling narrative that guides your audience through your presentation, making it more memorable and impactful.

Challenge 5: Neglecting practice and preparation

The saying *"practice makes perfect"* couldn't be truer when it comes to presentations. Preparation and rehearsal are key to delivering a polished and confident presentation. Take the time to rehearse your presentation multiple times, focusing on the timing, delivery, and flow. By doing so, you'll build confidence in conveying your message and ensure a smooth and engaging delivery.

Challenge 6: Ignoring audience engagement

A presentation should be a two-way interaction, not a monologue. Your audience wants to be engaged and involved. Incorporate interactive elements into your presentation, such as polls, Q&A sessions, or small group activities, to encourage participation and keep your audience engaged. By actively involving them, you create a more dynamic and memorable experience.

Challenge 7: Lack of flexibility and adaptability

No matter how well-prepared we are, unexpected situations can arise during a presentation. Being flexible and adaptable is essential. Embrace the unexpected, be open to feedback and questions, and make adjustments on the spot if necessary. By demonstrating your ability to adapt, you not only show your expertise but also build trust and credibility with your audience.

To end this section, remember that by being mindful of these challenges and implementing strategies to overcome them, you can elevate your presentations to new heights. Keep in mind that the goal is to deliver a compelling, engaging, and impactful presentation that leaves a lasting impression on. By being aware of these challenges and avoiding these common mistakes, consultants can enhance their presentation skills and ensure their message is effectively communicated, engaging, and impactful.

Exercises and Activities for Applying the Concepts

Imagine you're standing in front of a room full of clients, ready to deliver a presentation. You take a deep breath, feeling a mix of excitement and nerves. As you begin, you notice some of your audience members start to drift off or glance at their phones. You realize that capturing their attention and keeping them engaged is crucial. This realization sparks a desire within you to enhance your advanced presentation skills and find creative ways to connect with your audience.

Exercise 1: Storytelling Practice

We all love a good story, and incorporating storytelling techniques into your presentations can make them more engaging and memorable. To practice this skill, choose a recent project or experience and craft a compelling story around it. Focus on the key messages and emotions you want to convey. Think about the structure, characters, and plotline. Practice telling your story, paying attention to your tone, gestures, and timing. Consider recording yourself and seeking feedback to refine your storytelling skills further.

Exercise 2: Slide Makeover

Slides are a visual aid that can greatly enhance your presentations. However, poorly designed slides can be a distraction and hinder your message. For this exercise, select a presentation you have previously created and review the slides critically. Identify areas where the design can be improved - excessive text, cluttered visuals, or inconsistent formatting. Apply principles of good slide design, such as using clear and concise content, impactful visuals, and a consistent color scheme. Revamp your slides to create a visually appealing and effective presentation.

Exercise 3: Audience Interaction Simulation

Engaging with your audience is crucial for a successful presentation. To practice audience interaction, gather a group of colleagues or friends and simulate a presentation scenario. Choose a topic relevant to your consulting work and deliver a portion of your presentation. During the simulation, encourage audience participation by asking questions, facilitating discussions, or assigning small group activities. Pay attention to how you engage with your audience, listen actively, and adapt your content based on their responses. Reflect on the experience and identify areas for improvement.

These exercises are designed to help you apply the concepts of advanced presentation skills in your consulting daily practice. By practicing storytelling, improving slide design, and simulating audience interaction, you'll enhance your ability to deliver engaging and impactful presentations. Remember, the more you practice, the more confident and effective you'll become in capturing and holding your audience's attention. So, embrace these exercises and let your presentation skills shine!

Conclusion

To wrap-up, the Advanced Presentation Skills chapter has taken us on a journey to explore the fundamental principles and techniques of effective presentations. We learned about the importance of connecting with our audience, structuring our content for maximum impact, and utilizing technology and presentation tools to enhance our delivery. We also discussed common challenges and mistakes to avoid, such as lack of preparation, excessive reliance on slides, and failure to engage with the audience.

By honing our advanced presentation skills, we can captivate our audience, convey our message with clarity and confidence, and leave a lasting impression. Whether it's through storytelling, compelling slide design, or audience interaction, we have discovered practical strategies to elevate our presentations and become more persuasive communicators.

I also invite you to carry forward these newfound skills and apply them in your consulting practice. Embrace opportunities to present with impact and influence, knowing that your advanced presentation skills will set you apart as a consultant who can effectively convey complex ideas and win over clients.

In the next chapter, Chapter 10: Advanced Facilitation Skills, we will dive into the art of facilitation, a skill that is essential for leading effective meetings, workshops, and group discussions. We will explore facilitation techniques, tools, and strategies to foster collaboration, manage diverse perspectives, and guide groups towards impactful outcomes. Get ready to enhance your facilitation skills and become a catalyst for productive and engaging interactions.

So, let's move forward with enthusiasm and curiosity, as we continue our journey of mastering the art of consulting.

Chapter 10: Advanced Facilitation Skills

I hope you're ready to dive into the art of guiding and leading impactful discussions and meetings. But before we embark on this exciting journey, let me share a little story with you.

Picture this: I recently found myself in a room full of executives, all gathered for a critical strategic planning session. As the facilitator, it was my responsibility to guide the conversation, ensure everyone's voices were heard, and drive the group towards a shared vision. The stakes were high, and the pressure was on.

But here's the thing: facilitation isn't just about keeping time and managing the agenda. It's about creating an environment where collaboration flourishes, ideas are explored, and decisions are made collectively. And in that moment, I realized the true power of advanced facilitation skills.

By employing facilitation techniques and strategies, I was able to foster open dialogue, encourage diverse perspectives, and create a safe space for constructive debate. I guided the group through exercises that sparked creativity and critical thinking, allowing us to uncover innovative solutions to complex challenges.

This experience made me realize that advanced facilitation skills are essential for any consultant who wants to drive meaningful change, facilitate effective teamwork, and unleash the full potential of a group. Whether you're leading a workshop, facilitating a brainstorming session, or guiding a team through a decision-making process, your facilitation skills can make all the difference.

And so, in this chapter, we will explore the key principles, techniques, and tools that will help you become an advanced facilitator. We'll delve into the art of creating a collaborative environment, managing group dynamics, and guiding discussions towards actionable outcomes. You'll discover how to adapt your facilitation approach to different situations and audiences, and learn techniques to overcome challenges that may arise during facilitation.

So, get ready to expand your facilitation toolkit, boost your confidence in leading group discussions, and become a master of guiding meaningful interactions. By the end of this chapter, you'll be equipped with the skills to facilitate impactful meetings and workshops that drive results and leave a lasting impact.

So, let's jump right in and explore the fascinating world of advanced facilitation skills together. Get ready to unlock the potential of collaborative conversations and lead with confidence. Let's go!

Introduction to the Advanced Facilitation Skills

As I sit here, reflecting on my journey as a consultant, I can't help but recall a particular moment that forever changed my perspective on facilitation. It was a few years ago when I found myself leading a workshop with a group of senior executives who were known for their strong personalities and diverse opinions. The goal was to reach a consensus on a critical business decision, but the dynamics in the room were tense and adversarial.

In that moment, I realized that my basic facilitation skills were not enough to navigate this complex situation. I needed a deeper understanding of group dynamics, conflict resolution, and decision-making processes. That's when I delved into the world of advanced facilitation skills.

Advanced facilitation skills are like a secret superpower that consultants can develop to effectively guide group interactions and foster productive collaboration. It's about creating an environment where participants feel heard, valued, and empowered to contribute their ideas. Agile Consulting Methodology, with its focus on adaptability, collaboration, and continuous improvement, has played a significant role in popularizing advanced facilitation skills in the consulting world.

Advanced facilitation skills refer to the set of techniques, strategies, and abilities that go beyond basic facilitation. It involves creating an environment that fosters collaboration, effective communication, and productive group dynamics. Advanced facilitators possess a deep understanding of group dynamics and are skilled in guiding discussions, managing conflicts, and encouraging participation from all participants. They have the ability to navigate complex situations, facilitate decision-making processes, and ensure that meetings and workshops achieve their desired outcomes. Advanced facilitation skills empower consultants to effectively lead group interactions, inspire creativity and innovation, and drive consensus and action.

Key Concepts, Techniques, and Tools

I'm excited to dive into the world of advanced facilitation skills with you. Just like a skilled conductor leading an orchestra, advanced facilitation skills allow consultants to guide group interactions and orchestrate productive discussions. In this chapter, I'll share with you the key concepts, techniques, and tools that will empower you to become an effective facilitator.

The key concepts, techniques, and tools around advanced facilitation skills are designed to enhance the effectiveness of group interactions and enable consultants to guide discussions and decision-making processes. Here are some of the key elements:

Concept 1: Group dynamics

Let's start with understanding the importance of group dynamics. Imagine this: you're facilitating a workshop with a diverse group of individuals, each with their unique perspectives and communication styles. Understanding the dynamics at play is crucial to navigate through these differences and create an inclusive environment where everyone feels comfortable sharing their ideas.

Understanding how groups function and the dynamics at play is crucial for effective facilitation. This includes recognizing different personality types, communication styles, power dynamics, and conflict resolution strategies.

Group dynamics refers to the interactions and relationships among individuals within a group. Understanding group dynamics is crucial for consultants as it enables them to navigate through the complexities of group interactions and leverage them to achieve the desired outcomes. Here's how you can get the most out of group dynamics as a consultant:

Build rapport and establish trust: Create a positive and inclusive environment where everyone feels comfortable sharing their thoughts and opinions. Foster open communication and encourage active participation from all group members.

Recognize and leverage diversity: Each member of the group brings their unique perspectives, experiences, and expertise. Embrace this diversity and encourage the exploration of different viewpoints. By valuing diversity, you can tap into a wealth of ideas and insights that can lead to innovative solutions.

Foster collaboration: Encourage collaboration and teamwork among group members. Facilitate activities that promote collaboration, such as group discussions, brainstorming sessions, and collaborative problem-solving exercises. Encourage active listening, respect for diverse opinions, and a willingness to consider multiple perspectives.

Manage conflicts effectively: Conflict can arise within a group due to differences in opinions, goals, or approaches. As a consultant, it's important to address conflicts constructively and facilitate resolution. Foster open dialogue, active listening, and empathy to understand different viewpoints. Help the group find common ground and work towards mutually beneficial solutions.

Manage group dynamics: Pay attention to the dynamics at play within the group, such as power dynamics, communication styles, and decision-making processes. Actively manage these dynamics to ensure equal participation, effective communication, and a balanced distribution of responsibilities.

Facilitate effective communication: As a consultant, you play a crucial role in facilitating effective communication within the group. Encourage active listening, promote clear and concise communication, and ensure that all group members have an opportunity to express their thoughts. Use active facilitation techniques, such as summarizing key points, asking clarifying questions, and encouraging further discussion.

By understanding and leveraging group dynamics effectively, you can create a productive and collaborative environment that maximizes the potential of the group. It allows you to harness the collective intelligence, creativity, and problem-solving capabilities of the group, leading to better outcomes for your consulting engagements.

Concept 2: Active listening

Next, we'll explore the power of active listening. Picture yourself in a meeting, truly engaged in the conversation, not just hearing the words but also grasping the underlying emotions and perspectives. Being an active listener allows you to build trust, demonstrate empathy, and create a safe space for open and honest discussions.

Being an active listener is essential for facilitators. It involves not only hearing what participants say but also understanding their underlying perspectives, emotions, and needs. Active listening helps create an inclusive and respectful environment where everyone feels heard and valued.

Active listening is a fundamental communication skill that involves fully focusing on, understanding, and responding to the speaker. As a consultant, active listening is essential for building rapport, gaining insights, and fostering effective communication with clients. Here's how you can get the most out of active listening:

Be present: When engaging in a conversation with a client, be fully present and give your undivided attention. Avoid distractions and demonstrate genuine interest in what the speaker is saying.

Listen without judgment: Suspend judgment and avoid making assumptions or jumping to conclusions. Be open-minded and receptive to different perspectives, allowing for a more thorough understanding of the client's needs and concerns.

Show empathy: Put yourself in the client's shoes and try to understand their emotions and experiences. Empathy helps you establish a connection and build trust, creating a safe space for open and honest communication.

Use non-verbal cues: Non-verbal cues, such as maintaining eye contact, nodding, and using appropriate facial expressions, convey attentiveness and understanding. They show the speaker that you are actively listening and engaged in the conversation.

Paraphrase and clarify: Paraphrasing what the client has said and clarifying any uncertainties demonstrates that you are actively processing the information. This also helps ensure mutual understanding and avoids misinterpretation.

Ask probing questions: Ask relevant questions that delve deeper into the client's thoughts, feelings, and motivations. Probing questions encourage the client to expand on their ideas and provide more detailed information.

Provide feedback: Offer constructive feedback to the client, summarizing key points and reflecting back their thoughts and concerns. This confirms that you have understood their message and allows for further clarification if needed.

Practice reflective listening: Reflective listening involves summarizing and restating what the client has said in your own words. This technique not only shows your understanding but also allows the client to verify if you have accurately captured their message.

By actively listening, you enhance your ability to comprehend the client's needs, expectations, and challenges. This understanding forms the foundation for providing valuable insights, recommendations, and solutions. Remember, effective communication starts with active listening, and it is a skill that can be developed and refined through practice and conscious effort.

Concept 3: Effective questioning

As a facilitator, asking effective questions is an art. Imagine posing thought-provoking questions that spark deep insights and encourage participants to think critically. Whether it's using open-ended questions to explore possibilities, probing questions to dig deeper, or clarifying questions to ensure clarity, skillful questioning helps unlock the wisdom of the group.

Skillful facilitators know how to ask the right questions to provoke thoughtful discussions and encourage participants to share their insights. Open-ended questions, probing questions, and clarifying questions can help uncover different perspectives and generate meaningful dialogue.

Effective questioning is a skill that consultants can leverage to gather information, stimulate critical thinking, and facilitate meaningful discussions. It involves asking well-crafted questions that encourage deeper exploration, provoke insights, and elicit valuable responses from individuals or groups.

To get the most out of effective questioning as a consultant, here are some key strategies:

Prepare in advance: Before engaging in a meeting or consultation, take the time to prepare a list of relevant questions based on the objectives and desired outcomes. This ensures that your questions are focused and targeted.

Use open-ended questions: Open-ended questions encourage detailed and thoughtful responses, allowing individuals to express their opinions, share experiences, and provide insights. These questions typically start with words like *"how,"* *"what,"* or *"why"* and prompt participants to provide more than a simple yes or no answer.

Practice active listening: Effective questioning goes hand in hand with active listening. Pay close attention to the responses given by individuals and use their answers to guide your subsequent questions. This demonstrates that you are genuinely interested and engaged in the conversation.

Use probing questions: Probing questions are follow-up questions that help dig deeper into a topic or challenge assumptions. They encourage individuals to think more critically and consider different perspectives. Probing questions can be used to explore underlying motivations, potential risks, or alternative solutions.

Be neutral and non-judgmental: As a consultant, it's important to create a safe and non-threatening environment where individuals feel comfortable sharing their thoughts and ideas. Avoid using questions that sound judgmental or biased, and maintain an objective stance throughout the conversation.

Ask for clarification: Sometimes, it's necessary to ask clarifying questions to ensure that you fully understand the information being shared. This helps prevent misunderstandings and ensures that you have accurate and complete information to work with.

Balance curiosity and structure: While it's important to be curious and explore different angles, it's also essential to maintain a structured approach. Use a combination of open-ended and focused questions to guide the conversation and keep it on track towards achieving the desired outcomes.

By mastering the art of effective questioning, consultants can uncover valuable insights, facilitate collaborative problem-solving, and drive meaningful conversations with their clients. It is a powerful tool that allows consultants to gather information, explore possibilities, and generate innovative solutions to complex challenges.

Concept 4: Visual facilitation

Visual facilitation is another powerful tool in your facilitator's toolkit. Visual facilitation is a technique that involves using visual aids to enhance group interactions and foster better understanding and engagement. Imagine using visual aids like flipcharts or digital tools to make concepts come alive. Visuals help participants grasp complex information, connect ideas, and foster better understanding and engagement.

Visual facilitation techniques, such as mind mapping and graphic recording, can help participants visualize complex information and improve comprehension and engagement. As a consultant, incorporating visual facilitation can have several benefits for both you and your clients.

Firstly, visual facilitation helps to make complex information more accessible and understandable. By using visuals such as diagrams, charts, or illustrations, you can simplify complex concepts, break down information into digestible chunks, and make it easier for participants to grasp and retain key ideas.

Visuals also have a powerful impact on memory and recall. When information is presented visually, it activates different parts of the brain and can enhance participants' ability to remember and recall the content. This can be particularly useful when you want to leave a lasting impression or ensure that important concepts are retained by your audience.

Furthermore, visual facilitation promotes engagement and participation. When participants see their ideas or contributions visually represented, it creates a sense of ownership and validation. They are more likely to stay engaged and actively participate in the discussion when they see their thoughts being acknowledged and integrated into the visual representation.

To get the most out of visual facilitation as a consultant, here are a few tips:

Plan and prepare: Identify the key concepts or ideas that you want to visually represent. Create a visual plan or storyboard before the facilitation session to ensure that your visuals align with the objectives and flow of the discussion.

Use a variety of visual aids: Experiment with different types of visuals, such as flipcharts, whiteboards, sticky notes, or digital tools. Choose the appropriate visual aids based on the context and the preferences of the participants.

Keep it simple and clear: Avoid cluttering your visuals with too much information. Use simple and concise visuals that convey the main ideas effectively. Use colors, symbols, and icons to enhance understanding and create visual appeal.

Involve participants: Encourage participants to contribute to the visual representation. Invite them to add their ideas, insights, or drawings to the visual aids. This fosters a sense of collaboration and ownership among the participants.

Practice and refine: Like any skill, visual facilitation improves with practice. Take the time to practice creating visuals, experimenting with different techniques, and refining your visual facilitation approach. Seek feedback from participants and adjust your visuals based on their input.

By incorporating visual facilitation techniques into your consulting practice, you can enhance communication, foster engagement, and create a more impactful and memorable consulting experience for both you and your clients.

Concept 5: Facilitation techniques

Now, let's talk about facilitation techniques. Picture yourself using brainstorming sessions to generate creative ideas, guiding the group through consensus-building techniques to reach agreements, or employing problem-solving techniques to tackle complex challenges. These techniques empower participants to collaborate, innovate, and make informed decisions.

Advanced facilitators employ a variety of techniques to create a participatory and collaborative environment. These may include brainstorming, consensus-building, decision-making frameworks, problem-solving techniques, and process mapping.

Facilitation techniques refer to a set of methods and approaches used by a facilitator to guide group discussions, encourage participation, and foster collaboration. As a consultant, mastering facilitation techniques can greatly enhance your ability to effectively facilitate meetings, workshops, and group sessions. Here are some tips to get the most out of facilitation techniques:

Understand the group's objectives: Before applying any facilitation technique, make sure you have a clear understanding of the group's goals and desired outcomes. This will help you select the most appropriate techniques to achieve those objectives.

Create a safe and inclusive environment: Establish an atmosphere of trust and respect where participants feel comfortable sharing their ideas and opinions. Encourage open communication, active listening, and discourage judgment or criticism.

Prepare and plan: Prior to the facilitation session, prepare an agenda and determine the appropriate techniques to use at different stages. Plan how you will introduce the techniques, provide clear instructions, and manage time effectively.

Adapt to the group dynamics: Every group is unique, and their dynamics may change throughout the session. Be flexible and adapt your facilitation techniques based on the group's energy, engagement levels, and individual preferences.

Encourage participation: Use techniques such as brainstorming, round-robin, or small group discussions to ensure active participation from all attendees. Engage everyone in the discussion and encourage quieter participants to share their thoughts.

Manage conflicts constructively: Facilitation techniques can help manage conflicts and disagreements within a group. Use techniques such as active listening, paraphrasing, and consensus-building to address conflicts and guide the group towards resolution.

Use visual aids and tools: Visual aids, such as charts, diagrams, or digital tools, can enhance understanding and engagement. Incorporate visual facilitation techniques to make complex concepts more accessible and stimulate creativity.

Reflect and improve: After each facilitation session, take time to reflect on what worked well and areas for improvement. Seek feedback from participants and use it to refine your facilitation techniques for future sessions.

Remember, effective facilitation is a skill that develops with practice and experience. By continuously honing your facilitation techniques and adapting them to different contexts, you can create an environment that fosters collaboration, creativity, and meaningful outcomes for your clients.

Concept 6: Conflict resolution

Conflict resolution is an inevitable part of group interactions. Conflict resolution is the process of addressing and resolving conflicts or disagreements between individuals or groups. As a consultant, you will often encounter conflicts in your engagements, whether it's between team members, stakeholders, or clients. Effectively managing and resolving conflicts is essential for maintaining positive working relationships and achieving project success. Here are some ways to get the most out of conflict resolution as a consultant:

Understand the root causes: Take the time to understand the underlying reasons behind the conflict. This could involve active listening, gathering perspectives from all parties involved, and identifying the main issues at hand. By understanding the root causes, you can address them directly and work towards a resolution that addresses everyone's concerns.

Foster open communication: Encourage open and honest communication between the conflicting parties. Create a safe and non-judgmental space where individuals can express their thoughts and feelings. Actively listen to each person's perspective and validate their experiences. Facilitate constructive dialogue and encourage parties to find common ground.

Find win-win solutions: Aim for a solution that satisfies the interests and needs of all parties involved. Look for creative alternatives and brainstorm potential solutions together. By focusing on collaboration and seeking mutually beneficial outcomes, you can build consensus and foster a sense of ownership and commitment to the resolution.

Mediate with empathy and impartiality: As a consultant, you may need to act as a mediator in conflicts. Approach the role with empathy, understanding that each party has their own perspective and experiences. Remain impartial and avoid taking sides. Instead, focus on facilitating communication, promoting understanding, and guiding the parties towards finding a resolution.

Learn from conflicts: View conflicts as learning opportunities. Reflect on the conflicts you encounter and analyze how they could have been prevented or resolved more effectively. Use each conflict as a chance to improve your conflict resolution skills, refine your approach, and enhance your ability to manage conflicts in future engagements.

Remember, conflict resolution is not about eliminating all conflicts but rather about addressing them in a constructive and collaborative manner. By effectively managing conflicts, you can build trust, strengthen relationships, and create a positive working environment for all stakeholders involved in your consulting engagements. Last but not least, we'll dive further into conflict resolution and management techniques in a subsequent chapter; so, keep on reading!

Concept 7: Meeting management

Meeting management is the backbone of successful facilitation. Effective facilitation involves managing meeting logistics, setting clear objectives, establishing ground rules, and keeping discussions on track. Picture yourself creating clear agendas, establishing ground rules, managing time effectively, and ensuring that discussions stay focused and productive. Mastering meeting management techniques allows you to create an organized and purposeful space for meaningful conversations. Time management, agenda creation, and meeting facilitation techniques ensure that meetings are productive and achieve the desired outcomes.

And so, meeting management techniques refer to the strategies and practices used to effectively plan, organize, and conduct meetings. As a consultant, mastering these techniques is essential for ensuring that meetings are productive, efficient, and result-oriented. Here are a few key meeting management techniques and tips to get the most out of them:

Clear objectives and agenda: Before the meeting, clearly define the objectives and create an agenda that outlines the topics to be discussed and the time allocated for each item. This helps keep the meeting focused and ensures that all necessary topics are addressed.

Time management: Start the meeting on time and strictly adhere to the agenda to avoid wasting time. Assign time limits to each agenda item and use timekeeping techniques like a visible timer or countdown to keep the meeting on track.

Active facilitation: As the meeting facilitator, it's your responsibility to guide the discussion, encourage participation from all attendees, and manage any conflicts or disruptions. Create a supportive and inclusive environment that allows everyone to contribute their ideas and perspectives.

Engaging techniques: Incorporate interactive and engaging techniques to maintain participants' attention and involvement. This can include small group discussions, brainstorming sessions, or using visual aids to present information.

Effective communication: Encourage open and respectful communication among meeting participants. Listen actively, ask clarifying questions, and encourage everyone to express their thoughts and opinions. Use effective communication techniques such as paraphrasing or summarizing to ensure understanding and alignment.

Action-oriented outcomes: At the end of the meeting, clearly define action items, responsibilities, and deadlines. Ensure that decisions are documented and shared with the relevant stakeholders. Follow up on action items and provide updates in subsequent meetings.

Continuous improvement: Evaluate the effectiveness of the meeting by gathering feedback from participants. Use this feedback to identify areas for improvement and make necessary adjustments for future meetings.

By implementing these meeting management techniques, consultants can optimize the time and resources spent on meetings, foster collaboration, and drive meaningful outcomes. Effective meeting management enhances communication, engagement, and decision-making, ultimately leading to successful consulting engagements.

Remember, these key concepts, techniques, and tools work in tandem to create an environment where participants can collaborate, generate insights, and make informed decisions. Advanced facilitation skills empower consultants to guide group interactions effectively and facilitate successful outcomes in their consulting engagements. But let's move on, and talk examples!

Practical Examples

To illustrate the application of advanced facilitation skills, this section presents three practical examples. By analyzing these examples, you'll gain insights into how to adapt your facilitation approach to various groups and achieve desired results.

Example 1: Facilitating a Stakeholder Workshop

In one of my consulting projects, I was tasked with facilitating a stakeholder workshop for a client undergoing a major organizational change. The goal was to bring together key stakeholders from different departments to align on the vision, objectives, and action plan for the change initiative. As the facilitator, I used advanced facilitation skills to create a safe and collaborative space for open dialogue. I employed techniques like icebreakers, small group discussions, and visual tools to encourage active participation and generate meaningful insights. By guiding the discussion and ensuring equal representation of all stakeholders, we were able to achieve consensus and develop a comprehensive action plan that had buy-in from everyone involved.

Example 2: Leading a Cross-Functional Problem-Solving Session

During another consulting engagement, I was leading a cross-functional problem-solving session for a client facing a complex operational challenge. The session involved bringing together representatives from different departments to analyze the issue, identify root causes, and develop solutions. As the facilitator, I employed advanced facilitation skills to guide the group through a structured problem-solving process. I used techniques such as brainstorming, affinity diagramming, and consensus-building exercises to foster collaboration and harness the collective intelligence of the participants. By facilitating effective communication and maintaining focus on the desired outcomes, we were able to generate innovative solutions and develop an implementation plan that addressed the challenge at hand.

Example 3: Facilitating a Conflict Resolution Meeting

In a challenging consulting project, I was brought in to facilitate a conflict resolution meeting between two departments within a client organization. The conflict had been ongoing for some time and was affecting collaboration and productivity. As the facilitator, I needed to create a neutral and supportive environment where both parties felt comfortable expressing their concerns and finding common ground. I used advanced facilitation techniques such as active listening, reframing, and empathetic communication to help the participants understand each other's perspectives and find mutually agreeable solutions. Through open dialogue and a focus on finding win-win outcomes, we were able to successfully resolve the conflict and establish a framework for improved collaboration moving forward.

These real-world examples illustrate how advanced facilitation skills can be applied in various consulting scenarios to promote effective communication, collaboration, and problem-solving. By employing these skills, consultants can guide discussions, manage conflicts, and drive successful outcomes in complex and challenging situations.

Challenges and Common Mistakes to Avoid

As a consultant, I've experienced my fair share of challenges and mistakes when it comes to facilitating meetings and workshops. In this chapter, I want to share some personal anecdotes and insights to help you navigate the common challenges and avoid the pitfalls that can arise in facilitation sessions. So, let's dive in!

Challenge 1: Lack of Preparation

It was a bright Monday morning, and I was scheduled to facilitate a strategy workshop for a client. As I began the session, I realized I hadn't prepared enough. The lack of clarity about the objectives and agenda made it difficult to guide the discussion effectively. Lesson learned: Always invest time in thorough preparation, defining clear goals, designing appropriate activities, and ensuring you have the necessary materials and resources.

Challenge 2: Dominating or Disruptive Participants

In one particular facilitation session, I encountered a participant who seemed determined to dominate the conversation. They constantly interrupted others and disregarded their perspectives. To manage such situations, I quickly established ground rules at the beginning of the session, encouraging equal participation and setting clear expectations. By tactfully redirecting their behavior and ensuring everyone had an opportunity to contribute, we were able to maintain a positive and inclusive environment.

Challenge 3: Managing Time and Keeping Focus

During a lengthy facilitation session, I noticed that the discussions were going off track, and we were falling behind schedule. It was challenging to cover all the important topics adequately. To address this, I started setting clear timeframes for each agenda item, allocating sufficient time for key discussions, and using timekeeping techniques to stay on track. This allowed us to manage time effectively and ensure that we stayed focused on our objectives.

Challenge 4: Handling Resistance to Change

In a recent facilitation session centered around implementing a new process, I encountered resistance from some participants who were hesitant to embrace the change. To address this, I created a safe space for open dialogue, actively listened to their concerns, provided rationale for the change, and highlighted the benefits and opportunities it presented. By addressing their resistance and involving them in the decision-making process, we were able to overcome their objections and move forward collaboratively.

Challenge 5: Ineffective Communication

During a workshop with a diverse group of participants, I realized that miscommunications were hindering our progress. To enhance communication, I practiced active listening, used clear and concise language, employed visual aids and tools to enhance understanding, and encouraged open and respectful communication among participants. These strategies helped create a supportive and collaborative atmosphere, ensuring that everyone felt heard and understood.

Facilitation can be a challenging yet rewarding endeavor. By sharing my experiences and lessons learned, I hope to help you navigate the common challenges and avoid the mistakes that can hinder effective facilitation. Remember, with thorough preparation, effective communication, and a proactive approach to addressing challenges, you can become a skilled facilitator who fosters productive and meaningful discussions. In the next chapter, we will explore the essential skills and techniques for advanced facilitation. So, let's continue this journey together!

Exercises and Activities for Applying the Concepts

To enhance your advanced facilitation skills, let me provide you with three exercises for practice and application. These activities will enable you to practice facilitating different types of discussions, simulate challenging group dynamics, and refine your facilitation techniques.

Exercise 1: Role-play Scenarios

Set up role-play scenarios that simulate challenging facilitation situations. Assign different roles to participants, such as a disruptive participant, a resistant stakeholder, or a participant with strong emotions. Have participants practice their facilitation skills by effectively managing these scenarios. Afterwards, facilitate a group discussion to reflect on the strategies used and identify areas for improvement.

Exercise 2: Facilitation Observation and Feedback

Organize a group facilitation session where participants take turns facilitating a discussion on a specific topic. As each participant facilitates, others observe and take notes on their facilitation techniques, including their ability to engage participants, manage time, and handle challenging situations. After each facilitation session, provide constructive feedback to help participants refine their skills and identify areas for growth.

Exercise 3: Facilitation Techniques Brainstorming

Divide participants into small groups and assign each group a specific facilitation challenge, such as managing conflicts, encouraging participation, or fostering creativity. Ask each group to brainstorm and share facilitation techniques and strategies that could be used to address the challenge. After the brainstorming session, have each group present their ideas to the larger group, fostering a collaborative learning environment where participants can learn from each other's experiences and insights.

Remember, these exercises are designed to provide hands-on experience and reinforce the concepts of advanced facilitation skills. By actively engaging in these activities, participants can strengthen their facilitation abilities and develop a repertoire of techniques to apply in their consulting practice.

Conclusion

This chapter has explored the fundamental principles and concepts of facilitation in the context of consulting. We have seen how facilitation has gained popularity in the consulting world due to its ability to foster collaboration, drive effective decision-making, and enhance stakeholder engagement.

Throughout this chapter, we have delved into key concepts, techniques, and tools that can elevate your facilitation skills to the next level. We have discussed the importance of creating a safe and inclusive environment, active listening, managing group dynamics, and employing various facilitation techniques such as brainstorming, consensus-building, and problem-solving.

Additionally, we have examined the challenges and common mistakes to avoid when applying advanced facilitation skills, including managing difficult participants, maintaining impartiality, and ensuring effective time management. By being aware of these challenges and mistakes, you can navigate through them with confidence and professionalism.

To further reinforce your learning, we have provided practical examples that demonstrate the application of advanced facilitation skills in real-world consulting scenarios. These examples, experienced by our narrator, Cai, have highlighted the power of effective facilitation in driving productive meetings, resolving conflicts, and fostering innovation.

Lastly, we have suggested exercises and activities for you to practice and apply the concepts of advanced facilitation skills in your consulting daily practice. By engaging in role-play scenarios, observation and feedback sessions, and brainstorming exercises, you can hone your facilitation abilities and expand your repertoire of techniques.

As you continue your journey as a consultant, the advanced facilitation skills you have acquired will enable you to effectively guide and engage diverse stakeholder groups, drive meaningful discussions, and facilitate successful outcomes. Remember, facilitation is an ongoing process of learning and refinement, and with dedication and practice, you can become a masterful facilitator in your consulting practice.

Next, in Chapter 11, we will explore another crucial aspect of consulting: Executive Presence and Influence.

Chapter 11: Executive Presence and Influence

Picture this: It was a bright Monday morning, and I was about to step into the most important meeting of my consulting career. As I walked into the boardroom, filled with executives and decision-makers, I couldn't help but feel a mix of excitement and nervousness. This was my chance to make a lasting impression and influence the direction of the project.

As I sat down at the table, I observed the confident and commanding presence of the senior executives. They exuded an aura of authority and influence that instantly captivated the room. It was clear to me that they possessed something intangible yet immensely powerful – executive presence.

In that moment, I realized the importance of cultivating executive presence and influence as a consultant. It is not just about having the right skills and expertise, but also about how you carry yourself, communicate, and connect with others. Executive presence is about projecting confidence, credibility, and gravitas that commands attention and respect.

And so, in this chapter, I want us to explore the essential aspects of cultivating executive presence and harnessing the power of influence as a consultant. As a consultant, your ability to command attention, inspire trust, and influence key stakeholders is crucial to your success. Whether you're presenting a proposal to a client, leading a team, or engaging with senior executives, your executive presence and influence can significantly impact your outcomes.

Introduction to Executive Presence and Influence

Executive presence goes beyond just appearance; it encompasses a combination of confidence, credibility, communication skills, and the ability to build relationships. Executive presence refers to the ability to project confidence, credibility, and gravitas in a professional setting. It is about having a commanding presence that captures attention, instills trust, and inspires others. Executive presence is not solely based on one's position or title; it is a combination of qualities, behaviors, and communication skills that make an individual influential and impactful. By mastering the art of executive presence, consultants can establish themselves as trusted advisors and drive impactful change within organizations.

For a consultant, executive presence is especially important. It goes beyond technical expertise and knowledge. It is about how you carry yourself, how you engage with clients and stakeholders, and how you establish yourself as a trusted advisor. Executive presence allows consultants to effectively communicate their ideas, influence decision-making, and build strong relationships with clients and colleagues.

Having executive presence as a consultant means being able to exude confidence, professionalism, and credibility in every interaction. It means demonstrating strong communication skills, active listening, and empathy. It involves being aware of your body language, tone of voice, and overall demeanor. It also entails having a strategic mindset, being able to think on your feet, and presenting yourself as a trusted expert in your field.

By cultivating executive presence, consultants can enhance their ability to influence and make an impact on their clients and the organizations they work with. It helps them gain the respect and trust of key stakeholders, making it easier to navigate complex situations, gain buy-in for their recommendations, and ultimately drive successful outcomes.

In essence, executive presence and influence are critical components of a consultant's toolkit. They enable consultants to establish themselves as influential thought leaders, build strong relationships, and effectively guide organizations through change and transformation.

Key Concepts, Techniques, and Tools

As I walked into the boardroom, I couldn't help but feel a sense of anticipation and excitement. Today, I was going to present my proposal to a room full of senior executives. I knew that in order to succeed, I needed to have a strong executive presence and the ability to influence. But what does that mean exactly? Well, let us dive into the key concepts, techniques, and tools that contribute to building executive presence.

Concept 1: Self-awareness - Knowing Your Strengths and Areas for Growth

As consultants, we must have a deep understanding of ourselves to cultivate executive presence. It starts with self-awareness - recognizing our strengths, weaknesses, values, and beliefs. I've found that taking personality assessments and seeking feedback through 360-degree assessments can provide valuable insights into our leadership style and areas for improvement. By knowing ourselves, we can confidently navigate the challenges that come our way.

Self-awareness is the ability to recognize and understand our own strengths, weaknesses, values, and beliefs. As consultants, self-awareness is crucial as it allows us to leverage our strengths and address areas for growth, ultimately maximizing our potential. Here's how to get the most out of self-awareness as a consultant:

Reflect on your experiences: Take time to reflect on your past experiences, both successes and failures. Consider what you did well and what areas you could improve upon. This reflection helps you identify your strengths and areas for growth.

Seek feedback: Actively seek feedback from colleagues, supervisors, and clients. Constructive feedback can provide valuable insights into your performance, allowing you to understand how you are perceived by others. Be open to feedback and use it as an opportunity for growth.

Take assessments: Personality assessments, such as the Myers-Briggs Type Indicator (MBTI) or the DISC assessment, can provide insights into your personality traits, preferences, and working style. These assessments can help you understand how you interact with others and identify areas for development.

Engage in self-reflection: Regularly set aside time for self-reflection. Consider your values, beliefs, and motivations. Ask yourself what drives you and what areas you need to work on. Journaling or meditation can be helpful practices to enhance self-reflection.

Seek ongoing learning and development: Continuously seek opportunities for learning and growth. Attend workshops, webinars, or training programs that focus on self-awareness and personal development. Engaging in professional development activities can expand your knowledge and help you develop new skills.

Find a mentor or coach: Work with a mentor or coach who can provide guidance and support in your self-awareness journey. A mentor or coach can help you identify blind spots, set goals, and hold you accountable for your growth.

Remember, self-awareness is an ongoing process, and it requires a commitment to self-reflection and continuous learning. By developing a deep understanding of yourself, you can leverage your strengths, address areas for improvement, and ultimately excel in your consulting career.

Concept 2: Emotional Intelligence - Connecting with Others

Emotional intelligence (EI) is the ability to recognize, understand, and manage our own emotions while also empathizing with the emotions of others. As a consultant, developing strong emotional intelligence is crucial for building relationships, establishing trust, and influencing others effectively.

Emotional intelligence is a critical skill for building executive presence and influence. It involves understanding and managing our own emotions while empathizing with others. One technique I've honed is self-regulation - staying calm and composed even in high-pressure situations. Additionally, active listening and showing genuine empathy enable me to connect with others on a deeper level and build strong relationships.

Here's how you can get the most out of emotional intelligence in your consulting practice:

Self-Awareness: Start by developing a deep understanding of your own emotions, triggers, and patterns of behavior. Take time for self-reflection and explore how your emotions impact your decision-making and interactions with others. By becoming more self-aware, you can better regulate your emotions and respond effectively in different situations.

Empathy: Empathy is the ability to understand and share the feelings of others. Practice active listening and try to see things from the perspective of your clients, colleagues, and stakeholders. Cultivate empathy by seeking to understand their needs, concerns, and motivations. This will help you build rapport and establish strong connections with others.

Emotional Regulation: Emotionally intelligent consultants have the ability to manage their emotions, particularly in high-pressure or challenging situations. Practice techniques such as deep breathing, mindfulness, and self-talk to stay calm and composed. By regulating your emotions, you can make rational decisions, maintain professionalism, and positively influence those around you.

Social Skills: Building strong relationships and effective communication are key components of emotional intelligence. Enhance your social skills by practicing active listening, assertive communication, and conflict resolution. Develop your ability to express your thoughts and emotions clearly and respectfully. These skills will enable you to navigate difficult conversations, build trust, and collaborate effectively with clients and colleagues.

Continuous Learning: Emotional intelligence is a skill that can be developed and refined over time. Stay open to feedback and seek opportunities for growth and improvement. Reflect on your interactions and learn from both successes and failures. By continuously learning and adapting, you can enhance your emotional intelligence and strengthen your ability to connect with others.

Remember, emotional intelligence is not just about understanding emotions; it's about leveraging emotions to build meaningful connections and influence positive outcomes. By incorporating emotional intelligence into your consulting practice, you can establish strong relationships with clients, navigate complex situations, and drive impactful change.

Concept 3: Communication Skills - Conveying Ideas with Impact

Effective communication is key to executive presence. Communication skills are essential for consultants to convey their ideas effectively and make a lasting impact. When we can communicate clearly and persuasively, we can influence stakeholders, gain support for our proposals, and drive positive change.

Techniques such as clear and concise messaging, storytelling, and active listening can help us convey our ideas with impact. I've learned that crafting a compelling narrative and adapting my communication style to different audiences allows me to engage and influence effectively.

Here are some key strategies to get the most out of your communication skills as a consultant:

Craft a Compelling Narrative: To convey ideas with impact, it's crucial to structure your messages in a compelling narrative format. Begin with a strong opening that captures attention and clearly state your main points. Use storytelling techniques to make your ideas relatable and engaging. Paint a vivid picture of the desired outcome and explain how it aligns with the client's objectives.

Adapt to Your Audience: Effective communication requires understanding your audience and tailoring your message accordingly. Take the time to research your audience's background, interests, and communication preferences. Adapt your language, tone, and level of detail to resonate with their needs and expectations. This shows that you understand their perspective and builds rapport.

Use Visuals and Data: Visual aids and data can enhance the impact of your communication. Incorporate relevant visuals, such as charts, graphs, or infographics, to illustrate key points and make complex information more digestible. Data-driven evidence adds credibility to your arguments and helps stakeholders grasp the importance of your recommendations.

Active Listening: Communication is a two-way process, and active listening is a vital component. Show genuine interest in what others have to say, ask clarifying questions, and provide thoughtful responses. By actively listening, you demonstrate respect and create a collaborative atmosphere that fosters open dialogue and effective problem-solving.

Seek and Provide Feedback: Continuous improvement is key to enhancing your communication skills. Seek feedback from colleagues, mentors, or clients on your communication style and delivery. Actively incorporate the feedback received to refine your approach. Additionally, provide constructive feedback to others, as it promotes growth and strengthens relationships.

Practice, Practice, Practice: The more you practice your communication skills, the more comfortable and confident you become. Practice delivering presentations, engaging in discussions, and handling challenging conversations. Seek opportunities to speak in public or participate in group discussions to sharpen your communication abilities. Consider recording yourself and reviewing the footage to identify areas for improvement.

By honing your communication skills and leveraging these strategies, you can convey your ideas with impact and effectively influence your clients and stakeholders. Remember, effective communication is a fundamental skill that underpins successful consulting engagements, and it is worth investing time and effort to master this key concept.

Concept 4: Body Language and Nonverbal Communication - Making a Lasting Impression

Our body language and nonverbal cues play a significant role in how we are perceived. Techniques such as maintaining good posture, using appropriate gestures, and maintaining eye contact project confidence and credibility. By paying attention to these details, I've seen how my executive presence is enhanced, and my influence grows.

Body language and nonverbal communication refer to the messages conveyed through physical movements, gestures, facial expressions, and posture. It plays a crucial role in communication, as it can convey emotions, attitudes, and intentions that may not be expressed verbally. In the context of consulting, mastering body language and nonverbal communication skills is essential for making a lasting impression on clients and effectively conveying your message.

To get the most out of body language and nonverbal communication as a consultant, consider the following key aspects:

Awareness: Develop awareness of your own body language and nonverbal cues. Pay attention to your posture, facial expressions, and gestures. Being aware of how you present yourself nonverbally allows you to make intentional choices and align your nonverbal communication with your message.

Eye contact: Maintain appropriate eye contact during conversations and presentations. It shows confidence, engagement, and attentiveness. However, be mindful of cultural norms, as eye contact can vary across different cultures.

Facial expressions: Use facial expressions to convey emotions and show genuine interest and empathy. A warm smile, attentive look, and appropriate facial expressions can help build rapport and connect with clients on a deeper level.

Gestures and body movements: Utilize purposeful gestures to emphasize key points and illustrate concepts. However, be mindful of excessive or distracting movements that may detract from your message. Use open and relaxed body language to appear approachable and confident.

Posture: Maintain an upright and confident posture during meetings and presentations. Avoid slouching or crossing your arms, as it may signal defensiveness or disinterest. Standing or sitting tall conveys professionalism and assertiveness.

Active listening: Nonverbal cues are also important for effective listening. Use nodding, leaning forward, and maintaining an open body posture to show attentiveness and engagement. This encourages clients to feel heard and understood.

Adaptability: Be aware of cultural differences in body language and nonverbal communication. Different cultures may interpret nonverbal cues differently, so it's important to adapt your approach accordingly. Research and learn about the cultural norms and practices of your clients to avoid misunderstandings.

To enhance your skills in body language and nonverbal communication as a consultant, consider the following strategies:

- Video record yourself during practice sessions or presentations. Review the recordings to observe your nonverbal cues and identify areas for improvement.
- Seek feedback from trusted colleagues or mentors who can provide constructive criticism and suggestions for enhancing your nonverbal communication skills.

- Attend workshops or training sessions on body language and nonverbal communication to learn specific techniques and strategies for effectively utilizing nonverbal cues in professional settings.

By developing your body language and nonverbal communication skills, you can make a lasting impression on clients, establish trust, and effectively convey your expertise and message in the consulting field.

Concept 5: Building Relationships and Networking - Expanding Your Circle of Influence

Building strong relationships and networks is essential for executive presence and influence. Actively participating in professional communities, attending networking events, and cultivating relationships with key stakeholders allows us to expand our influence and gain support for our ideas. These connections are invaluable in propelling our consulting careers forward.

Building strong relationships and expanding our circle of influence is a crucial aspect of executive presence and influence as a consultant. It involves connecting with others, establishing rapport, and cultivating networks that support our professional growth. Here are some strategies to get the most out of building relationships and networking:

Actively participate in professional communities: Join industry associations, attend conferences, and engage in online forums relevant to your consulting niche. Actively contribute to discussions, share insights, and seek opportunities to connect with like-minded professionals. By immersing yourself in these communities, you can expand your network and gain valuable industry knowledge.

Attend networking events: Take advantage of networking events to meet potential clients, industry leaders, and fellow consultants. Come prepared with a clear elevator pitch and be genuinely interested in learning about others. Be open to initiating conversations and follow up with meaningful interactions after the event. Remember, building relationships takes time and effort.

Cultivate relationships with key stakeholders: Identify key decision-makers, influencers, and stakeholders within your client organizations. Take the initiative to connect with them, either through formal meetings or informal interactions. Show genuine interest in their challenges, goals, and aspirations. By building rapport and trust with these individuals, you can expand your influence within the organization.

Share your expertise and provide value: Offer your insights, knowledge, and expertise generously. Write articles or blog posts, speak at industry events, or contribute to relevant publications. By establishing yourself as a thought leader, you attract the attention of potential clients and build credibility within your field. Be willing to share your experiences and help others succeed.

Nurture relationships over time: Building lasting relationships requires consistent effort. Follow up with contacts regularly, whether through emails, phone calls, or face-to-face meetings. Stay informed about their professional endeavors and find ways to offer support or collaboration. By maintaining these connections, you can establish a network of trusted individuals who can vouch for your capabilities and refer new opportunities to you.

Seek mentors and advisors: Identify experienced consultants or industry veterans who can provide guidance and support. These mentors can offer valuable insights, share their experiences, and help you navigate challenges in your consulting career. Actively seek their advice and apply their wisdom to your own professional development.

By actively building relationships and expanding your network, you can broaden your circle of influence as a consultant. These connections can lead to new business opportunities, referrals, and collaborative partnerships. Remember to approach networking with authenticity, sincerity, and a genuine interest in helping others. Building lasting relationships is not just about what you can gain, but also about how you can contribute to the success of others in your network.

Concept 6: Executive Image and Personal Branding - Creating a Lasting Impression

In the world of consulting, our executive image and personal branding play a significant role in how we are perceived by clients, colleagues, and stakeholders. It's about creating a lasting impression that reinforces our expertise, professionalism, and value. Let's dive into this key concept and explore how to get the most out of it as a consultant.

Our executive image and personal branding contribute to our overall presence and influence. Dressing professionally, developing a personal brand, and managing our online presence are techniques that can enhance our credibility and influence.

Firstly, executive image refers to the way we present ourselves physically and professionally. As consultants, we must dress professionally, taking into account the expectations of our clients and the industry we work in. Dressing appropriately not only demonstrates respect but also helps to establish credibility and professionalism.

To get the most out of your executive image, it's important to understand the expectations and norms of your consulting engagements. Consider the dress code, cultural considerations, and the level of formality expected in different situations. By adapting your image to align with the client's expectations, you can establish a positive first impression and build rapport more easily.

Personal branding, on the other hand, is about how we position ourselves and communicate our unique value proposition. As consultants, our personal brand should reflect our expertise, strengths, and the specific value we bring to our clients. It's about creating a distinctive identity that sets us apart from others in the field.

To maximize the impact of your personal branding, start by clarifying your professional strengths and the unique value you offer. Identify your areas of expertise, the results you have achieved for clients, and the specific skills or knowledge that differentiate you. Use this understanding to craft a clear and compelling personal brand statement that communicates your value succinctly and persuasively.

In today's digital age, managing your online presence is also crucial for executive image and personal branding. Ensure that your professional profiles, such as LinkedIn, accurately represent your skills, experience, and achievements. Share valuable content, engage with industry thought leaders, and maintain a consistent online presence that aligns with your personal brand.

To get the most out of your executive image and personal branding as a consultant, it's essential to be authentic and consistent. Your image and brand should be aligned with your values and reflect who you truly are as a professional. Authenticity builds trust and credibility, which are vital for establishing lasting relationships with clients.

Lastly, seek feedback and continuously refine your executive image and personal branding. Ask for input from trusted colleagues, mentors, and clients to gain insights into how you are perceived and how you can enhance your image and brand. Take the feedback constructively and make adjustments as necessary to strengthen your presence and influence.

By focusing on your executive image and personal branding, you can create a lasting impression that aligns with your expertise, establishes credibility, and differentiates you as a consultant. It's a powerful tool that can enhance your professional reputation and open doors to exciting opportunities. Last, by carefully curating our image, we leave a lasting impression that reinforces our expertise and value as consultants.

Concept 7: Power and Influence Strategies - Navigating Complex Situations

In the world of consulting, we often find ourselves in complex and challenging situations where navigating power dynamics and exerting influence are crucial for success. Key Concept 7 focuses on power and influence strategies that can help us effectively navigate these complexities and achieve our goals. Understanding power dynamics and influence strategies is crucial in our consulting engagements. Building coalitions, utilizing persuasive communication, and honing negotiation skills are techniques that help us navigate complex situations and gain buy-in for our ideas.

To get the most out of this concept as a consultant, it's important to understand the following:

Power dynamics: Recognize the sources of power within an organization or among key stakeholders. This includes formal power (position or authority) and informal power (expertise, relationships, or influence). By understanding the power dynamics at play, you can strategically position yourself and align your influence efforts.

Building coalitions: Identify and cultivate relationships with key individuals or groups who can support your initiatives. Building alliances and coalitions can amplify your influence and create a united front when facing resistance or challenges.

Persuasive communication: Master the art of persuasive communication to effectively convey your ideas and gain buy-in from others. Tailor your message to the needs and interests of your audience, highlight the benefits and impact of your proposals, and use compelling arguments and evidence to support your case.

Negotiation skills: Develop strong negotiation skills to navigate conflicts and reach mutually beneficial outcomes. This involves understanding the interests and priorities of all parties involved, finding common ground, and creatively exploring win-win solutions.

Managing resistance: Anticipate and address potential resistance to your ideas or proposals. Actively listen to concerns, address objections with empathy and logic, and seek to find solutions that address the underlying issues. By actively managing resistance, you can build trust and increase the likelihood of successful implementation.

Influencing without authority: Learn to influence others even when you don't have formal authority. This requires building credibility, demonstrating expertise, and developing strong relationships. By gaining the trust and respect of others, you can effectively influence decisions and outcomes.

To get the most out of power and influence strategies as a consultant, remember to approach each situation with authenticity, integrity, and a focus on achieving mutually beneficial outcomes. By mastering these strategies, you can navigate complex situations, overcome obstacles, and drive meaningful change within your consulting engagements. By mastering these strategies, we can exert our influence effectively and drive meaningful change.

Developing executive presence and influence is an ongoing journey that requires continuous self-reflection and refinement of skills. By combining self-awareness, emotional intelligence, effective communication, body language, relationship building, personal branding, and power and influence strategies, we can unlock our full potential as consultants.

Practical Examples

To illustrate the application of executive presence and influence, allow me to tell you about two of my recent experiences.

Example 1: Influencing a Senior Stakeholder

As a consultant working on a strategic project for a large organization, I found myself needing to influence a senior stakeholder who held significant decision-making power. This stakeholder had a different perspective on the project and was resistant to the proposed changes. To navigate this situation, I applied executive presence and influence strategies.

First, I invested time in understanding the stakeholder's priorities and concerns. I conducted research, had conversations with other team members, and sought insights from those who had interacted with this stakeholder in the past. This helped me gain valuable information about their preferences and motivations.

Armed with this knowledge, I approached the stakeholder with a well-prepared and tailored communication strategy. I framed my proposals in a way that aligned with their interests and emphasized the benefits and positive impact of the changes. I used data and evidence to support my arguments and showcased successful case studies from similar organizations.

Additionally, I worked on building a relationship of trust and credibility with the stakeholder. I actively listened to their concerns and addressed them with empathy and respect. I sought their input and feedback, making them feel valued and included in the decision-making process. By consistently demonstrating my expertise and integrity, I earned their respect and trust over time.

Through effective communication, building relationships, and demonstrating a strong executive presence, I was able to influence this senior stakeholder to reconsider their initial resistance. They eventually became an advocate for the proposed changes and played a crucial role in driving the project's success.

Example 2: Navigating Interdepartmental Dynamics

In another consulting engagement, I was tasked with facilitating a project that required collaboration among multiple departments within an organization. The challenge was that these departments had a history of conflict and competition, making it difficult to achieve alignment and cooperation.

To navigate these interdepartmental dynamics, I employed executive presence and influence strategies. I began by facilitating open and transparent communication channels among the departments. I encouraged them to voice their concerns, interests, and goals, creating a safe space for dialogue and collaboration.

Next, I focused on finding common ground and shared objectives among the departments. I conducted workshops and brainstorming sessions where we explored their mutual challenges and opportunities. By highlighting how their individual goals could be achieved more effectively through collaboration, I fostered a sense of shared purpose and encouraged buy-in from all parties.

Throughout the process, I proactively managed resistance by addressing conflicts and tensions as they arose. I facilitated discussions to resolve disagreements and sought win-win solutions that meet the needs of all departments. By fostering a sense of fairness and inclusivity, I built trust and cooperation among the teams.

As the project progressed, the executive presence and influence strategies I employed helped transform the interdepartmental dynamics. The departments started working collaboratively, sharing resources, and leveraging each other's strengths. The project achieved its objectives, and the improved interdepartmental relationships continued beyond the engagement, benefiting the organization as a whole.

These examples demonstrate how executive presence and influence can be applied in real-life consulting scenarios to drive alignment, build relationships, and overcome resistance. By utilizing these strategies effectively, consultants can navigate complex situations, gain support for their ideas, and achieve successful outcomes in their engagements.

Challenges and Common Mistakes to Avoid

As a consultant, I've come to realize that executive presence and influence play a crucial role in achieving success in the consulting world. It's not just about having the knowledge and expertise, but also about effectively navigating complex situations and influencing key stakeholders. In this chapter, I want to share with you some of the common challenges and mistakes to avoid when it comes to executive presence and influence.

Challenge 1: Lack of Self-awareness

Picture this: I was once assigned to a high-stakes project with a challenging client. At the time, I didn't fully understand my own strengths, weaknesses, and biases. I soon realized that this lack of self-awareness was hindering my ability to effectively influence others. It was a valuable lesson to learn that self-awareness is key to managing my behavior and influencing stakeholders successfully.

Challenge 2: Insufficient Understanding of Stakeholders

Let me tell you about a time when I was working on a project with multiple stakeholders. I made the mistake of not investing enough time to understand their needs, motivations, and concerns. As a result, my communication and influence strategies were ineffective. It became clear that to make an impact, I needed to take the time to truly understand my stakeholders and tailor my messages and strategies accordingly.

Challenge 3: Overreliance on Positional Power

Early in my consulting career, I believed that my job title alone would give me the power and influence I needed. However, I soon realized that true influence goes beyond positional power. It requires building credibility, trust, and expertise. It was a humbling experience to learn that influence is earned, not granted, and that I needed to focus on developing these qualities to effectively influence stakeholders.

Challenge 4: Ineffective Communication

Imagine this: I was in a meeting with senior executives, and I found myself struggling to communicate my ideas effectively. I was using jargon, speaking too fast, and failing to listen actively. It became evident that clear and concise communication, adapted to the needs of the audience, was essential for successful influence. I made a conscious effort to improve my communication skills, and it made a significant difference in my ability to influence others.

Challenge 5: Neglecting Relationship Building

Let me share a story about a project where I neglected to build strong relationships with key stakeholders. I focused solely on delivering results, overlooking the importance of building rapport and trust. This mistake resulted in resistance and lack of support from stakeholders. I learned the hard way that investing time and effort in building relationships is crucial for effective influence.

Challenge 6: Lack of Flexibility and Adaptability

In my consulting journey, I encountered many unexpected challenges and resistance. Initially, I was resistant to change and found it difficult to adapt my approach. However, I soon realized that flexibility and adaptability are essential for successful influence. Being open to feedback, adjusting strategies, and finding alternative approaches became my mantra, enabling me to navigate complex situations more effectively.

Challenge 7: Failure to Influence Upward

Once, I found myself struggling to influence senior leaders on a project. It was intimidating, and I wasn't sure how to gain their buy-in. Through trial and error, I learned to navigate power dynamics and adapt my approach to effectively influence decision-makers. It was a valuable lesson that taught me the importance of understanding and tailoring my influence strategies to different stakeholders.

By being aware of these challenges and avoiding common mistakes, consultants can enhance their executive presence and influence skills. This will enable them to navigate complex consulting environments, build strong relationships with stakeholders, and achieve successful outcomes in their engagements.

Exercises and Activities for Applying the Concepts

To develop and enhance your executive presence and influence, consider the below activities. They will help you refine your communication skills, strengthen your ability to build rapport with senior leaders, and develop strategies for influencing decision-making processes.

Exercise 1: Reflect and Self-Assess

Take some time to reflect on your own executive presence and influence. Ask yourself questions such as: How do I come across to others? What strengths do I possess that contribute to my influence? What areas do I need to improve upon? Consider seeking feedback from colleagues or mentors to gain additional insights. Use this self-assessment to identify areas for growth and development.

Exercise 2: Role-Playing Scenarios

Engage in role-playing exercises to practice and refine your executive presence and influence skills. Create scenarios that simulate real-life consulting situations, such as presenting a recommendation to a client or influencing a difficult stakeholder. Act out these scenarios with a colleague or mentor, and take turns playing different roles. Pay attention to your communication style, body language, and ability to adapt your approach to different stakeholders. This exercise will help you gain confidence and enhance your ability to influence effectively.

Exercise 3: Build a Network

Networking is a valuable tool for developing executive presence and influence. Identify key individuals within your professional network who have strong executive presence and influence skills. Seek opportunities to connect with them, whether through industry events, conferences, or online communities. Engage in conversations, ask for advice, and learn from their experiences. Building relationships with influential individuals can provide you with guidance, support, and opportunities for growth.

Remember, these exercises are designed to help you apply the concepts of executive presence and influence in your consulting practice. By actively engaging in these activities, you can strengthen your skills, expand your influence, and ultimately achieve greater success in your consulting career.

Conclusion

In conclusion, the chapter on executive presence and influence explored the essential concepts, techniques, and tools that consultants can utilize to enhance their presence and influence in the business world. We discussed the importance of building credibility, establishing a strong personal brand, and developing effective communication skills.

We learned that executive presence goes beyond mere appearance; it encompasses the way we carry ourselves, communicate, and interact with others. By cultivating a confident and authentic presence, consultants can inspire trust and establish themselves as influential leaders.

We also explored various strategies for building influence, such as leveraging relationships, understanding power dynamics, and employing persuasive techniques. We emphasized the importance of adapting our communication style to different stakeholders and effectively navigating complex situations.

Throughout the chapter, we highlighted common challenges and pitfalls to avoid, including lack of self-awareness, overconfidence, and failure to adapt to diverse audiences. By being mindful of these challenges, consultants can better navigate their professional interactions and maximize their influence.

To further enhance our executive presence and influence, we engaged in practical exercises and activities, such as self-assessment, role-playing scenarios, and building a strong professional network. By actively applying these concepts, we can continuously refine our skills and develop a powerful presence in the consulting field.

Remember, executive presence and influence are not static qualities but are skills that can be developed and honed over time. By embracing the principles discussed in this chapter, consultants can elevate their impact, gain the trust and respect of clients and stakeholders, and achieve success in their consulting careers.

With the knowledge and insights gained from this chapter, we are now prepared to move forward and explore the next topic: advanced business strategy. In the upcoming chapter, we will delve into the intricacies of strategic thinking, planning, and execution, equipping ourselves with the tools and techniques necessary to navigate complex business challenges and drive sustainable growth.

So, let's continue this exciting journey together as we expand our consulting toolkit and elevate our capabilities to new heights...

Chapter 12: Storytelling for Consulting

Imagine this scenario: you are in a meeting with a group of clients, eager to present your latest consulting recommendations. You have done your research, prepared the slides, and gathered all the necessary data. But as you start speaking, you notice that your audience is becoming disengaged. Their eyes glaze over, and you can sense their attention slipping away.

Feeling a wave of frustration, you wonder why your presentation, which is filled with valuable insights and recommendations, isn't resonating with your audience. That's when you realize the missing ingredient: storytelling.

In this chapter, we will explore the fascinating world of storytelling for consulting. Storytelling is not just about spinning a good yarn; it is a powerful tool that consultants can harness to captivate their audience, evoke emotions, and drive impactful change.

I have always been a firm believer in the power of storytelling, and I've seen firsthand how it can transform a dull presentation into an unforgettable experience. Let me share a personal anecdote that highlights the impact of storytelling in a consulting context.

A few years ago, I was tasked with helping a struggling retail company regain its competitive edge. The company's leadership was disheartened, and the employees were demotivated. I knew that to truly connect with them and inspire change, I needed to go beyond charts and graphs. I needed to tell a story.

During my presentation, I painted a vivid picture of the company's history, starting from its humble beginnings and highlighting the challenges it had overcome. I wove in personal narratives of employees who had experienced firsthand the company's highs and lows. I shared anecdotes that illustrated the struggles and triumphs of the retail industry.

As I spoke, I could see a shift in the room. The energy changed, and the audience became engaged. They leaned in, eager to hear what would happen next. Through storytelling, I was able to convey not just facts and figures, but emotions and aspirations.

By the end of the presentation, the leadership team was inspired, and the employees felt a renewed sense of purpose. The power of storytelling had ignited a spark within them, motivating them to embrace change and work towards a brighter future.

And so, let's dive into the key concepts, techniques, and tools that will enable you to harness the power of storytelling in your consulting practice.

Introduction to the Storytelling for Consulting

Storytelling for consulting is the practice of using narratives to convey complex information, engage stakeholders, and influence decision-making. It involves crafting and delivering compelling stories that resonate with your audience, evoke emotions, and drive meaningful change.

Storytelling is important for consultants for several reasons. First, it helps consultants connect with their audience on a deeper level. When you tell a story, you tap into the power of human emotion and create a memorable experience. This enables you to engage stakeholders, build trust, and make a lasting impact.

Second, storytelling allows consultants to simplify complex concepts and data. By weaving facts and figures into a narrative, you make information more relatable and understandable. This is crucial in the consulting world, where clients often face complex challenges and need to make informed decisions.

Third, storytelling helps consultants inspire action and drive change. Through stories, you can create a vision of the desired future, articulate the benefits of your recommendations, and address potential objections. By engaging the hearts and minds of your audience, you increase the likelihood of them embracing your ideas and taking action.

Furthermore, storytelling helps consultants differentiate themselves and stand out in a competitive market. When you can convey your expertise and insights through compelling stories, you leave a lasting impression on clients and stakeholders. This sets you apart from other consultants who rely solely on technical jargon and data-driven presentations.

In essence, mastering the skill of storytelling allows consultants to communicate with impact, build strong relationships, and drive meaningful change. It enables them to connect with their audience, simplify complex information, inspire action, and differentiate themselves in a crowded consulting landscape. By incorporating storytelling into their practice, consultants can elevate their effectiveness and achieve greater success in their engagements.

Key Concepts, Techniques, and Tools

It's late and I am starting to be a little tired. So, please, allow me get to the point.

Concept 1: Story Structure - Crafting Compelling Narratives

Story structure refers to the framework and organization of a narrative. It is the backbone that holds the story together and guides the audience through a cohesive and engaging experience.

But, let me share a story with you. I had always been fascinated by the power of storytelling and its ability to captivate audiences. As a consultant, I knew that mastering the art of storytelling was essential to effectively communicate ideas and influence stakeholders. And so, I embarked on a journey to understand the key concept of story structure. In this section, we will explore the fundamental elements of a compelling story. Just like any good story, a consultant's narrative needs a clear beginning, middle, and end. I learned that a well-defined protagonist, such as a client or a business, can drive the story forward. Additionally, a central conflict or challenge sets the stage for the consulting engagement and creates a compelling narrative arc.

As a consultant, understanding story structure is crucial for crafting compelling narratives that effectively communicate your message and resonate with stakeholders. Here are some key points to get the most out of story structure:

Introduction and Set-Up: Begin by setting the stage and introducing the main characters or context of the story. Clearly establish the problem or challenge that needs to be addressed, creating intrigue and capturing the audience's attention from the start.

Conflict and Rising Action: Develop the story by presenting obstacles, conflicts, or challenges that the characters face. This creates tension and keeps the audience engaged. Show the journey of how the problem evolved and escalated, highlighting the significance and implications of the situation.

Climax and Resolution: Reach a turning point in the story where the tension peaks and the main conflict is confronted. This is the pivotal moment where the resolution or outcome is determined. Clearly articulate the actions taken, decisions made, and results achieved to resolve the problem or address the challenge.

Lessons Learned and Takeaways: Conclude the story by reflecting on the lessons learned and the key takeaways for the audience. Share insights, observations, and the impact of the resolution. Emphasize the value and relevance of the story to the consulting context, highlighting how it relates to the client's situation or the overall objective of the engagement.

To get the most out of story structure as a consultant, consider the following tips:

Understand Your Audience: Tailor your story structure to the specific needs, interests, and preferences of your audience. Adapt the storytelling approach based on their level of understanding, background knowledge, and expectations.

Keep it Concise and Focused: Be mindful of the time constraints and attention spans of your audience. Craft a story structure that is concise, focused, and to the point. Eliminate any unnecessary details or tangents that may distract from the core message.

Use Visual Aids and Supporting Materials: Enhance your storytelling by incorporating visual aids, such as charts, graphs, or images, that help illustrate key points and make the narrative more visually engaging. Consider using multimedia tools, such as videos or interactive presentations, to enhance the impact of your story.

Practice and Refine: Like any skill, storytelling requires practice and refinement. Rehearse your storytelling techniques to ensure a smooth and confident delivery. Seek feedback from colleagues or mentors to identify areas for improvement and refine your story structure for maximum impact.

By mastering story structure and applying these tips, you can effectively engage your audience, communicate complex ideas, and leave a lasting impression as a consultant. Storytelling becomes a powerful tool in your consulting toolkit, enabling you to connect with stakeholders, inspire action, and drive meaningful change.

Concept 2: Audience Analysis - Tailoring Stories for Impact

Now, let's dive into the next key concept: audience analysis. Cai quickly realized that the success of a story depends on its resonance with the intended audience. Cai discovered the importance of understanding the needs, interests, and level of understanding of the audience. By conducting thorough audience analysis, Cai could tailor the storytelling approach to ensure relevance and engagement.

Audience analysis is the process of understanding the characteristics, needs, preferences, and expectations of your audience in order to tailor your stories for maximum impact. As a consultant, getting the most out of audience analysis is crucial for effective storytelling. Here's how you can do it:

Research and gather information: Before crafting your story, conduct thorough research on your audience. Understand their background, knowledge level, interests, and values. Use various sources such as interviews, surveys, and market research to gather insights that will help you tailor your story accordingly.

Identify key pain points and objectives: By understanding your audience's challenges, pain points, and objectives, you can align your story with their needs. This allows you to address their concerns and provide relevant solutions or insights that resonate with them.

Adapt your storytelling style: Tailor your storytelling style to match the preferences and communication styles of your audience. Consider factors such as their level of expertise, cultural background, and industry norms. For example, if your audience consists of technical experts, you may need to use more technical language and provide detailed data.

Use relatable examples and analogies: Make your story relatable by incorporating examples and analogies that your audience can easily understand and connect with. This helps to bridge any knowledge gaps and ensures that your message is easily digestible and memorable.

Incorporate visual aids and multimedia: Use visual aids, such as charts, graphs, or videos, to enhance your storytelling and make complex information more accessible. Visuals can help your audience grasp concepts more effectively and enhance their engagement with your story.

Engage in active listening: During your storytelling, pay attention to your audience's reactions and body language. Adjust your pace, tone, and content based on their responses. Active listening allows you to gauge the level of engagement and adapt your storytelling approach accordingly.

I learned that different stakeholders might have varying levels of knowledge about the consulting topic at hand. Therefore, I developed the ability to adapt the story's language, tone, and complexity to effectively communicate with different audiences. Whether it was presenting to executives, frontline staff, or a mix of stakeholders, my storytelling prowess was flexible and adaptable. So, trust me, when I said that by applying audience analysis techniques, you can tailor your stories to have a powerful impact on your consulting clients. By understanding their needs, preferences, and challenges, you can create stories that resonate with them, capture their attention, and inspire action.

So, when preparing your next consulting presentation, take the time to analyze your audience and customize your stories to make a lasting impression. Your ability to connect with and influence your audience through tailored storytelling will set you apart as a consultant.

Concept 3: Emotional Connection - Engaging Hearts and Minds

Imagine a moment when I stood in front of a room full of skeptical stakeholders. I knew that to capture their attention and gain their support, an emotional connection was essential. I discovered that storytelling was a powerful tool to evoke emotions and create that connection. I learned to incorporate personal anecdotes, relatable characters, and vivid descriptions to bring the story to life. By sharing the human side of the consulting journey, I could touch the hearts of the audience and foster empathy. I understood that by engaging both the hearts and minds of stakeholders, the impact of the story would be profound.

Emotional connection is the ability to engage the hearts and minds of your audience by evoking emotions and creating a meaningful connection with them. As a consultant, mastering emotional connection is crucial because it helps build trust, rapport, and buy-in from your clients and stakeholders. Here are some key strategies to get the most out of emotional connection as a consultant:

Know your audience: Understanding your audience is essential to establish an emotional connection. Conduct thorough research and gather insights about their needs, values, and aspirations. This knowledge will enable you to tailor your messages and stories to resonate with their emotions.

Storytelling: Harness the power of storytelling to create emotional connections. Share personal experiences, anecdotes, or client success stories that evoke emotions and relate to the challenges or aspirations of your audience. Craft narratives that are relatable, authentic, and impactful, and use storytelling techniques such as vivid descriptions, compelling characters, and well-structured plots to engage your audience emotionally.

Use visual and nonverbal cues: Nonverbal communication plays a significant role in creating emotional connections. Pay attention to your body language, facial expressions, and tone of voice to convey your emotions and intentions. Additionally, leverage visual aids such as images, videos, or infographics to enhance the emotional impact of your messages.

Empathy and active listening: Demonstrate empathy by actively listening to your clients and stakeholders. Show genuine interest in their perspectives, concerns, and needs. By understanding their emotions and responding with empathy, you can establish a deeper connection and build trust.

Authenticity and vulnerability: Be authentic and genuine in your interactions. Share your own emotions and vulnerabilities when appropriate, as this can create a sense of relatability and authenticity. It shows that you are a real person with real emotions, making it easier for others to connect with you on an emotional level.

Tailor your communication style: Adapt your communication style to resonate with the emotional preferences of your audience. Some individuals may respond more to logical and analytical arguments, while others may be more influenced by stories and personal experiences. Flex your communication approach to meet the emotional needs of your stakeholders.

By incorporating these strategies into your consulting practice, you can create powerful emotional connections that foster trust, engagement, and collaboration with your clients and stakeholders. Remember, emotional connection goes beyond the rational aspects of consulting and taps into the human side, making it a critical skill for success in the field.

Concept 4: Framing and Messaging - Delivering Key Insights

As I progressed in the consulting world, the importance of framing and messaging became evident. I realized that storytelling was not just about telling a good story; it was about delivering key insights and recommendations. I also learned to structure the story in a way that emphasized the desired takeaways. By carefully framing the narrative around the central message, I could guide the audience's understanding and influence their perspectives. I still have a long way to go to master the art of presenting insights in a compelling and persuasive manner, ensuring that the story left a lasting impact, but I'm making progress daily, and so could you.

Framing and messaging refers to the art of delivering key insights in a way that captures the attention of the audience and influences their perception. As a consultant, mastering this skill is crucial for effectively communicating recommendations and driving desired outcomes. Here are some tips on how to get the most out of framing and messaging as a consultant:

Understand your audience: Before delivering your message, take the time to understand the needs, priorities, and perspectives of your audience. Tailor your framing and messaging to resonate with their interests and values, ensuring that your insights are relevant and impactful to them.

Craft a compelling narrative: Use storytelling techniques to frame your insights in a compelling and relatable narrative. Start with a clear and attention-grabbing introduction, present your key insights in a logical and structured manner, and conclude with a memorable and actionable call-to-action.

Use language effectively: Choose your words carefully to convey your message concisely and powerfully. Use simple and jargon-free language to ensure clarity and understanding. Use persuasive language to influence the audience's perception and motivate action.

Emphasize the benefits: Clearly articulate the benefits and value of your insights to the audience. Show how your recommendations can solve their problems, improve efficiency, increase profitability, or achieve their goals. Highlight the positive outcomes they can expect from adopting your recommendations.

Support your insights with evidence: Back up your insights with credible data, research, case studies, or examples. This provides credibility to your message and helps build trust with your audience. Use visuals or other supporting materials to enhance the clarity and impact of your message.

Practice and refine: Practice delivering your framing and messaging in various scenarios. Seek feedback from trusted colleagues or mentors and incorporate their suggestions. Continuously refine your approach to make your messaging more persuasive, concise, and impactful.

By mastering the art of framing and messaging, you can effectively deliver key insights that resonate with your audience, influence their perception, and drive positive outcomes for your consulting engagements.

Concept 5: Visual Aids and Multimedia - Enhancing the Storytelling Experience

Visual aids and multimedia refer to the use of visual elements and digital media to enhance the storytelling experience. As a consultant, leveraging visual aids and multimedia can significantly amplify the impact of your stories and engage your audience on a deeper level.

To get the most out of visual aids and multimedia as a consultant, consider the following:

Choose the right visual aids: Select visual aids that align with the message and tone of your story. This could include slides, charts, graphs, images, videos, or infographics. Ensure that the visuals are relevant, clear, and visually appealing.

Use multimedia strategically: Incorporate multimedia elements such as videos, audio clips, or animations to enhance the storytelling experience. Multimedia can bring your stories to life, evoke emotions, and make complex concepts more understandable.

Keep it simple and concise: Avoid overwhelming your audience with too many visuals or excessive information. Keep the visual aids and multimedia elements simple, concise, and easy to grasp. Use visuals to support your narrative rather than distract from it.

Practice and synchronize: Familiarize yourself with the visuals and multimedia you plan to use. Practice your presentation to ensure smooth transitions between your spoken words and the visuals. Synchronize your storytelling with the visual aids to create a seamless and engaging experience.

Adapt to the audience and context: Consider the preferences and needs of your audience when using visual aids and multimedia. Adjust your approach based on the setting, culture, and technological capabilities available. Be mindful of any accessibility considerations and ensure everyone can fully engage with the visual content.

By effectively incorporating visual aids and multimedia into your storytelling, you can capture your audience's attention, enhance their understanding, and leave a lasting impression. Remember, visual aids and multimedia are powerful tools that can elevate your storytelling and help you connect with your audience on a deeper level.

Concept 6: Storytelling Techniques - Captivating and Engaging Audiences

Storytelling techniques are the various methods and approaches used to captivate and engage audiences when delivering a story. As a consultant, mastering these techniques is crucial for effectively communicating ideas, influencing stakeholders, and making a lasting impact. Here are some key aspects to get the most out of storytelling techniques:

Structure and Narrative Flow: Craft your story using a clear structure, such as the classic beginning, middle, and end. Build a narrative flow that takes the audience on a journey, incorporating elements like an engaging introduction, a compelling conflict, and a satisfying resolution.

Emotion and Connection: Infuse your story with emotion to create a connection with your audience. Use vivid descriptions, relatable characters, and personal anecdotes to evoke feelings and engage their empathy. This emotional connection enhances the impact of your message and makes it more memorable.

Visual and Verbal Communication: Employ a combination of visual aids, such as slides, images, or props, and verbal communication to enhance your storytelling. Use visuals to support key points, create visual metaphors, or provide visual cues that reinforce the narrative. Your voice modulation, tone, and gestures should align with the story's mood and purpose.

Audience Relevance: Tailor your story to the specific needs and interests of your audience. Understand their background, motivations, and challenges to ensure that your story resonates with them. Make the content relevant by drawing parallels to their experiences and highlighting the benefits or insights that matter to them.

Simplicity and Clarity: Keep your story concise and easy to understand. Use simple language, avoid jargon, and eliminate unnecessary details. Clarity is key to ensuring that your message is understood and remembered by your audience.

Practice and Delivery: Rehearse your storytelling to become comfortable and confident in delivering your narrative. Practice speaking with clarity, maintaining eye contact, and using appropriate pacing. Pay attention to your body language and use it to enhance your storytelling.

By applying these storytelling techniques, consultants can capture their audience's attention, convey complex ideas in a relatable manner, and inspire action. Remember to practice, seek feedback, and adapt your storytelling approach based on the unique needs of each situation and audience.

Concept 7: Authenticity and Connection - Building Trust and Rapport

From the get-go, I understood that authenticity played a vital role in effective storytelling. By being genuine and true to oneself, I could build trust and rapport with the audience. And so, I learned that sharing personal experiences, vulnerabilities, and lessons learned created a sense of authenticity that resonated with stakeholders. This connection fostered a deeper level of engagement and made the storytelling experience more impactful.

Authenticity and Connection - Building Trust and Rapport is a key concept in storytelling for consulting. It involves being genuine, honest, and establishing a connection with the audience to build trust and rapport. As a consultant, mastering authenticity and connection is essential for effectively delivering messages and influencing stakeholders.

To get the most out of authenticity and connection as a consultant, there are a few techniques and strategies to consider:

Be genuine and true to yourself: Authenticity starts with being true to who you are as a consultant. Embrace your unique experiences, perspectives, and values. When you are genuine, it creates a sense of trust and credibility with your audience.

Share personal experiences: Sharing personal stories and experiences can be a powerful way to connect with others. These stories can help illustrate key points, make your message relatable, and show vulnerability. Sharing personal experiences can also demonstrate that you understand the challenges your clients are facing.

Listen actively and show empathy: Building connection and rapport requires active listening and empathy. Truly understanding your clients' needs, concerns, and aspirations will help you tailor your storytelling to resonate with them. Show empathy by acknowledging their emotions and demonstrating that you genuinely care about their success.

Use storytelling techniques to engage emotions: Emotional connections are key to building trust and rapport. Use storytelling techniques such as vivid imagery, compelling characters, and relatable narratives to evoke emotions in your audience. When people feel emotionally engaged, they are more likely to remember and connect with your message.

Build relationships over time: Building trust and rapport is an ongoing process. Take the time to cultivate relationships with your clients, colleagues, and stakeholders. Consistently delivering on your promises, being reliable, and demonstrating integrity will strengthen the connection and trust you have with others.

By embracing authenticity, sharing personal experiences, actively listening, showing empathy, and using storytelling techniques to engage emotions, you can build trust and rapport as a consultant. This will enhance your ability to connect with your audience, influence their perspectives, and drive meaningful change.

Concept 8: Practice and Feedback - Refining the Art of Storytelling

Practice and Feedback - Refining the Art of Storytelling involves dedicating time and effort to perfecting your storytelling skills and seeking feedback to improve. As a consultant, getting the most out of this process can greatly enhance your storytelling abilities. Here's how to make the most of practice and feedback:

Embrace regular practice: Set aside dedicated time to practice storytelling. Create a routine where you can develop and refine your storytelling techniques. Practice in front of a mirror, record yourself, or enlist a trusted colleague or mentor to be your practice audience. The more you practice, the more comfortable and confident you will become in delivering compelling stories.

Seek constructive feedback: Feedback is crucial for growth and improvement. Share your storytelling with others and actively seek their feedback. Ask for specific insights on your delivery, clarity, engagement, and overall impact. Encourage honest feedback and be open to suggestions for improvement. Embrace feedback as an opportunity to refine your storytelling skills.

Reflect and refine: After each storytelling practice session or presentation, take time to reflect on your performance. Identify areas where you excelled and areas that could use improvement. Analyze your storytelling structure, pacing, tone, and emotional connection with the audience. Use this reflection to refine your storytelling approach for future engagements.

Incorporate feedback into future practices: Apply the feedback you receive to your future storytelling practices. Use the insights gained to make adjustments and enhancements to your delivery and storytelling techniques. Continuously iterate and refine your storytelling based on the feedback you receive.

By consistently practicing and seeking feedback, you can refine your storytelling skills and elevate your ability to engage and influence your audience as a consultant. Remember, storytelling is a craft that requires ongoing effort and improvement. Embrace the process, be open to feedback, and continue to refine your storytelling artistry to become a masterful storyteller in the consulting realm.

By understanding the power of story structure, conducting audience analysis, creating emotional connections, framing and messaging effectively, leveraging visual aids and multimedia, employing storytelling techniques, and embracing authenticity, consultants can master the art of storytelling.

So, as you embark on your own storytelling journey, remember to practice, seek feedback, and stay true to your authentic voice. The ability to tell compelling stories will elevate your consulting practice, enabling you to engage, influence, and inspire stakeholders.

Practical Examples

Alright, to illustrate the power of storytelling in consulting, let me share with you two stories…

Example 1: The Power of a Compelling Story

I was working with a client in the technology industry who was struggling to gain buy-in from my stakeholders for a new product launch. The client had all the data and information to support the product's potential, but I was failing to connect with my audience on an emotional level. I decided to incorporate storytelling into my presentation.

During the presentation, I shared a story about how the product had transformed the life of an individual, painting a vivid picture of their struggles and the positive impact the product had made. By weaving this narrative throughout the presentation, I was able to captivate the audience and convey the product's value in a relatable and memorable way. As a result, the client successfully secured the support I needed, all thanks to the power of storytelling.

Example 2: Building Trust through Personal Stories

In another consulting engagement, I was working with a client who was experiencing internal resistance to change. The employees were skeptical about the proposed changes and were hesitant to embrace them. I realized that in order to build trust and inspire confidence in the change initiative, I needed to connect with the employees on a personal level.

During a town hall meeting, I shared a personal story about a time I faced a similar challenge and how I overcame it. This story allowed me to establish a connection with the audience and demonstrate empathy for their concerns. By sharing my own vulnerabilities and lessons learned, I was able to inspire the employees to embrace the change with a renewed sense of trust and confidence.

These examples highlight how storytelling can be a powerful tool for consultants. By crafting and delivering compelling stories, consultants can engage their audience, convey complex information in a relatable way, and build trust and rapport. Storytelling allows consultants to connect with their clients and stakeholders on a deeper level, ultimately driving greater success in their consulting engagements.

Challenges and Common Mistakes to Avoid

Storytelling for consulting can come with its own set of challenges, and this section will address common pitfalls and mistakes to avoid.

Challenge 1: The Importance of Relevant Stories

In the beginning, let me share a story with you. Picture this: I was sitting in a client meeting, excited to present my findings and recommendations. As I began my presentation, I decided to start with a story that I thought was fascinating. However, as I delved into the details, I noticed confusion and disinterest on the faces of my audience. It hit me then that I had made a common mistake - I had chosen a story that wasn't directly relevant to the topic at hand.

The key concept here is the importance of using relevant stories in your consulting engagements. Stories that align with your message and resonate with your audience have a powerful impact. By choosing stories that directly relate to the topic, you can capture your audience's attention and make your message more memorable.

Challenge 2: The Art of Simplicity

Let me take you back to another client meeting, where I was eager to impress with a complex and intricate story. However, as I noticed confusion growing on the faces of my audience, I realized that I had fallen into a common trap - overcomplicating the storytelling process.

The key concept here is the art of simplicity. When crafting your stories, strive to keep them simple, focused, and aligned with your key points. Remember that your audience needs to grasp your message easily, so clear and concise storytelling is essential. By simplifying your stories, you can engage your audience and help them connect with your message more effectively.

Challenge 3: The Power of Authenticity

Let me share a personal experience that taught me the importance of authenticity in storytelling. In a high-stakes client meeting, I chose to share a story that I thought would impress and establish my credibility. However, the lack of authenticity was apparent, and it created a disconnect with my audience.

The key concept here is the power of authenticity. When telling stories, draw from genuine personal experiences or real-life situations. Authentic storytelling builds trust and credibility with your audience, allowing them to connect with you on a deeper level. By being true to yourself and sharing stories that reflect your own journey, you can create a more meaningful impact.

Challenge 4: Eliciting Emotional Appeal

Imagine this: I was in a boardroom, presenting a critical proposal to a group of stakeholders. As I shared a story that lacked emotional appeal, I noticed disengagement and a lack of enthusiasm in the room. It became clear to me that I had neglected the emotional aspect of storytelling.

The key concept here is the importance of eliciting emotional appeal in your stories. Emotions have the power to captivate and inspire. By incorporating emotions into your storytelling, you can create a deeper connection with your audience, making your message more impactful and memorable.

Challenge 5: Crafting Structure and Flow

Let me take you back to a presentation I gave, where I had neglected the structure and flow of my story. As I jumped between different points and lacked a clear narrative structure, I noticed the audience's attention wavering.

The key concept here is the significance of crafting structure and flow in your stories. A well-structured story has a clear beginning, middle, and end. It should have a compelling opening, build tension or intrigue, and conclude with a powerful message or call to action. By paying attention to the narrative flow, you can ensure that your stories engage and hold your audience's attention throughout.

In conclusion, storytelling is a powerful tool for consultants to communicate and influence effectively. By being aware of these challenges and avoiding these common mistakes, consultants can effectively leverage storytelling techniques to enhance their communication and influence, making a more significant impact on their clients and stakeholders.

Exercises and Activities for Applying the Concepts

To strengthen your storytelling skills and apply the concepts discussed in this chapter, let me give you homework! Here are two exercises that can help the reader apply the concepts of storytelling for consulting in their daily practice:

Exercise 1: Storytelling Practice Sessions

Instructions:
- Choose a topic or consulting scenario: Select a topic or consulting scenario relevant to your work or industry. It could be a case study, a client presentation, or a problem-solving situation.
- Craft a story: Create a story that connects to the chosen topic or scenario. Ensure that the story has a clear structure, a compelling opening, and a strong message or call to action.
- Practice telling the story: Rehearse telling the story out loud. Focus on your delivery, pacing, and emotional engagement. Pay attention to your body language, facial expressions, and voice modulation.
- Seek feedback: Share your story with a trusted colleague, mentor, or friend. Ask for their feedback on the clarity, relevance, and impact of the story. Incorporate their suggestions to improve your storytelling skills.

Exercise 2: Storytelling Reflection Journal

Instructions:

- Reflect on your consulting experiences: Take a few minutes each day to reflect on your consulting experiences. Identify key moments, challenges, or successes that can be transformed into compelling stories.
- Write in your journal: Write down these moments in your storytelling reflection journal. Describe the situation, the key characters involved, and the lessons learned or insights gained.
- Analyze and refine your stories: Periodically review your journal entries and analyze the stories you've captured. Look for opportunities to refine and improve them by adding relevant details, emotional appeal, or a clear message.
- Share your stories: Look for appropriate opportunities to share your stories in client meetings, presentations, or team discussions. Practice storytelling in a variety of contexts to strengthen your skills and influence.

These exercises will help you apply the concepts of storytelling for consulting in a practical and hands-on way, allowing you to refine your storytelling skills and make a greater impact in your consulting practice.

Conclusion

"Stories have power. They delight, enchant, touch, teach, recall, inspire, motivate, challenge. They help us understand. They imprint a picture on our minds. Want to make a point or raise an issue? Tell a story." - Janet Litherland

In conclusion, storytelling is a powerful tool that consultants can leverage to communicate ideas, engage clients, and drive meaningful change. In this chapter, we explored key concepts, techniques, and tools related to storytelling for consulting. We learned that effective storytelling involves understanding the audience, crafting compelling narratives, and using visual aids to enhance impact. We also discussed the importance of practice and feedback to refine storytelling skills.

Storytelling allows consultants to connect with their clients on an emotional level, making complex concepts more relatable and memorable. It helps build trust, credibility, and influence, as clients are more likely to engage with and act upon stories that resonate with them. By mastering storytelling, consultants can effectively convey their expertise, inspire action, and drive successful outcomes.

However, there are challenges and common mistakes to avoid when applying storytelling techniques. These include losing sight of the main message, overwhelming the audience with excessive information, and failing to adapt stories to different contexts. By being aware of these challenges, consultants can strive to overcome them and deliver impactful storytelling experiences.

To apply the concepts of storytelling in your daily consulting practice, consider engaging in practice sessions and seeking feedback from trusted colleagues. Additionally, keep a storytelling reflection journal to capture key moments and lessons learned. By honing your storytelling skills and sharing compelling stories, you can create lasting connections, influence stakeholders, and achieve greater success as a consultant.

Now, let's move on to the next chapter: Chapter 13: Advanced Negotiation Skills. In this chapter, we will delve into the world of negotiation, exploring strategies, techniques, and tools to navigate complex business situations and achieve win-win outcomes. Get ready to unlock your negotiation prowess and become a master of collaborative problem-solving.

Chapter 13: Advanced Negotiation Skills

Picture this. I found myself in a high-stakes negotiation with a client, desperately trying to strike a deal that would benefit both parties. The tension was palpable as we sat across the table, each side firmly defending their interests. The pressure was on, and I knew that my ability to negotiate effectively could make or break the outcome of this crucial engagement.

In that intense negotiation, I realized the importance of advanced negotiation skills. It's not just about haggling over prices or terms; it's about finding common ground, building relationships, and creating win-win solutions. As consultants, negotiation is an integral part of our daily interactions with clients, stakeholders, and team members. Whether it's securing a contract, resolving conflicts, or influencing decisions, negotiation skills are essential to achieving favorable outcomes.

Now, you might be wondering, what exactly are advanced negotiation skills? Well, buckle up, because we're about to explore the fundamental principles and concepts that underpin successful negotiations. We will uncover strategies, techniques, and tools that can give you the upper hand and help you navigate even the most complex negotiation scenarios.

But first, let's talk about why mastering advanced negotiation skills is so crucial for us as consultants. The consulting world is dynamic and ever-changing, and the ability to negotiate effectively can make or break a deal, influence client decisions, and ultimately determine the success of our projects. By honing our negotiation skills, we can enhance our ability to communicate persuasively, foster collaboration, and achieve mutually beneficial outcomes.

So, get ready to level up your negotiation game!

Introduction to Advanced Negotiation Skills

Negotiation is a fundamental skill for consultants, as it plays a crucial role in resolving conflicts, reaching agreements, and achieving mutually beneficial outcomes with clients and stakeholders. Whether you're negotiating project scope, fees, or terms, mastering advanced negotiation skills will empower you to navigate complex situations and secure favorable outcomes for both parties involved.

Advanced negotiation skills refer to a set of techniques, strategies, and mindset that go beyond the basics of negotiation. It involves a deeper understanding of the negotiation process and the ability to navigate complex situations, build relationships, and create mutually beneficial outcomes.

For a consultant, advanced negotiation skills are paramount in their daily work life. As consultants, we are often faced with challenging negotiations, whether it's negotiating project terms, contracts, fees, or resolving conflicts with clients or stakeholders. Advanced negotiation skills enable us to effectively communicate our ideas, influence decisions, and find win-win solutions that satisfy both parties' interests.

By mastering advanced negotiation skills, consultants can enhance their ability to:

Influence outcomes: Consultants often find themselves in situations where they need to influence decisions or gain buy-in from clients or stakeholders. Advanced negotiation skills help consultants to effectively persuade others, build trust, and influence outcomes in their favor.

Navigate complex situations: The consulting world can be intricate, and negotiations can become intricate as well. Advanced negotiation skills equip consultants with the ability to navigate through complex situations, such as multiple stakeholders with conflicting interests, challenging contractual terms, or sensitive discussions. It enables consultants to handle these complexities with finesse and find creative solutions.

Build strong relationships: Successful consulting often relies on building strong relationships with clients and stakeholders. Advanced negotiation skills involve effective communication, active listening, and understanding the needs and motivations of the other party. By building rapport and trust through skilled negotiation, consultants can foster long-term relationships that benefit both parties.

Create win-win outcomes: Advanced negotiation skills go beyond a zero-sum approach where one party wins and the other loses. Instead, it focuses on creating win-win outcomes that address the interests and concerns of all parties involved. By finding common ground and exploring mutually beneficial solutions, consultants can establish trust and cooperation with their clients, leading to successful collaborations.

In summary, advanced negotiation skills are a crucial asset for consultants in their daily work life. These skills empower consultants to influence decisions, navigate complex situations, build strong relationships, and create win-win outcomes. By honing these skills, consultants can achieve better results, build credibility, and enhance their overall effectiveness as trusted advisors to their clients.

Key Concepts, Techniques, and Tools

In this section, we will dive into the key concepts, techniques, and tools that will enhance your negotiation prowess. You'll learn about the importance of preparation and setting clear objectives before entering a negotiation. We'll explore strategies for effective communication, active listening, and building rapport with the other party. Additionally, we'll discuss various negotiation tactics, such as creating value, finding win-win solutions, and managing difficult conversations. You'll also discover tools and frameworks that can support your negotiation process, including BATNA (Best Alternative to a Negotiated Agreement) analysis and ZOPA (Zone of Possible Agreement) identification.

As a consultant, negotiation is an essential part of your daily work life. Whether you're working with clients, vendors, or colleagues, your ability to negotiate effectively can make a significant impact on the success of your projects and relationships.

Concept 1: Preparation - The Foundation of Successful Negotiations

Imagine this scenario: You have a crucial negotiation coming up with a prospective client. The outcome of this negotiation could determine the success of your project and the future of your consulting business. How do you prepare?

Thorough preparation is a critical component of negotiation success. It involves gathering information, analyzing data, and understanding the interests and motivations of all parties involved. As a consultant, here's how you can get the most out of thorough preparation:

Research and Gather Information: Before entering a negotiation, conduct thorough research on the topic at hand. Understand the industry, market trends, and relevant data that can impact the negotiation. Gather information about the other party, their needs, and their negotiation style.

Define Your Objectives and Priorities: Clearly define your objectives and priorities for the negotiation. Identify your desired outcomes and the key points you want to address. Consider both short-term and long-term goals and how they align with your client's objectives.

Identify Interests and Needs: Determine the interests and needs of all parties involved. Look beyond the surface-level positions and uncover the underlying motivations. This understanding will help you find common ground and explore potential trade-offs.

Develop a Strategy: Based on your research and understanding of the situation, develop a negotiation strategy. Determine the approach you will take, the tactics you will use, and the concessions you are willing to make. Anticipate potential challenges and plan how to address them.

Practice Effective Communication: Effective communication is essential in negotiation. Practice active listening skills to understand the other party's perspective. Develop clear and persuasive arguments to support your position. Prepare responses to potential objections or counterarguments.

Anticipate and Plan for Different Scenarios: Anticipate different scenarios and outcomes that may arise during the negotiation. Prepare alternative strategies and plans based on these scenarios. Being flexible and adaptable will enable you to navigate unexpected twists and turns.

Role-Play and Mock Negotiations: Consider conducting role-plays and mock negotiations to practice your negotiation skills. Engage with colleagues or friends to simulate realistic negotiation scenarios. This will help you refine your approach, test different strategies, and build confidence.

Stay Updated and Informed: Continuously monitor developments and changes that may impact the negotiation. Stay updated on market trends, industry news, and any relevant updates from the other party. This will help you adjust your approach and stay prepared throughout the negotiation process.

By investing time and effort into thorough preparation, you position yourself for negotiation success. It allows you to enter negotiations with confidence, clarity, and a solid understanding of the situation. This preparation sets the stage for effective communication, creative problem-solving, and ultimately, achieving favorable outcomes for your clients.

Concept 2: Effective Communication - Building Bridges and Finding Common Ground

Negotiation is all about communication. How you articulate your points, listen to the other party, and build rapport can greatly impact the outcome of your negotiations. Let's uncover the secrets of effective communication in negotiation.

Effective communication is a key aspect of advanced negotiation skills. It involves building bridges, finding common ground, and effectively conveying your message to the other party. As a consultant, mastering effective communication is crucial for achieving successful negotiation outcomes and building strong client relationships.

To get the most out of effective communication as a consultant, consider the following strategies:

Active Listening: Engage in active listening by giving your full attention to the other party. Truly understanding their needs, concerns, and perspectives is essential for finding common ground and developing mutually beneficial solutions. Avoid interrupting and show genuine interest in what they have to say.

Clear and Concise Communication: Use clear and concise language to convey your message effectively. Avoid jargon or technical terms that may confuse or alienate the other party. Structure your thoughts logically and present your ideas in a concise and easily understandable manner.

Nonverbal Communication: Pay attention to your nonverbal cues, such as body language, facial expressions, and tone of voice. Maintain eye contact, use appropriate gestures, and project confidence and professionalism. Nonverbal cues can significantly impact the message you convey and the impression you make.

Empathy and Emotional Intelligence: Develop empathy and emotional intelligence to understand the emotions and perspectives of the other party. Acknowledge and validate their feelings, and strive to establish a connection based on trust and understanding. This will help build rapport and facilitate open and constructive communication.

Building Rapport and Trust: Foster a positive and trustworthy relationship with the other party through effective communication. Show respect, authenticity, and integrity in your interactions. Building rapport and trust can lead to smoother negotiations and increased collaboration.

Adapting Communication Styles: Recognize that different individuals have different communication styles. Adapt your communication approach to meet the needs and preferences of the other party. This may involve adjusting your tone, level of formality, or communication medium to establish effective communication.

Feedback and Clarification: Seek feedback and clarification throughout the negotiation process. Regularly check for understanding and ask clarifying questions to ensure that both parties are on the same page. This helps to avoid misunderstandings and promotes effective communication.

By applying these strategies, you can enhance your ability to communicate effectively during negotiations as a consultant. Effective communication not only helps you convey your ideas and interests clearly but also enables you to understand and address the concerns and needs of the other party, leading to more successful negotiation outcomes.

Concept 3: The Power of Active Listening

Active listening is a superpower in negotiation. In this subsection, we'll explore how active listening can help you understand the other party's perspective, identify their interests, and build trust. I'll share stories of how active listening transformed challenging negotiations into successful partnerships.

The Power of Active Listening refers to the ability to fully engage and comprehend what the other party is saying during a conversation or negotiation. As a consultant, active listening is a crucial skill that can greatly enhance your effectiveness in client interactions and ultimately lead to better outcomes.

To get the most out of active listening as a consultant, consider the following:

Be fully present: When engaging in a conversation with a client, be fully present and give them your undivided attention. Put away distractions, such as your phone or laptop, and focus on the speaker. Show genuine interest and maintain eye contact to convey your attentiveness.

Listen actively: Active listening involves more than just hearing the words spoken. It requires actively processing and understanding the information being communicated. Practice active listening by paraphrasing or summarizing the speaker's points to ensure that you have accurately understood their message.

Ask probing questions: By asking thoughtful and open-ended questions, you can delve deeper into the client's thoughts and uncover valuable insights. This not only shows your engagement but also helps you gather more information to provide tailored solutions.

Empathize and show empathy: Empathy is a key component of active listening. Put yourself in the client's shoes and try to understand their perspective, needs, and concerns. Respond with empathy and validate their feelings to build trust and rapport.

Avoid interrupting or jumping to conclusions: It is important to refrain from interrupting the speaker or jumping to conclusions prematurely. Allow the client to fully express themselves before providing your input. This demonstrates respect and helps you gain a comprehensive understanding of their needs.

Take notes: Taking notes during the conversation can help you retain important information and show that you value the client's input. Jot down key points, concerns, and any action items discussed. This will also aid in effective follow-up and ensure that you address all relevant points.

Practice reflection and self-awareness: After the conversation or negotiation, take time to reflect on your listening skills. Evaluate how well you listened, any biases or assumptions that may have influenced your understanding, and areas for improvement. Continuously develop your self-awareness and strive to become an even better listener.

By mastering the power of active listening, you can establish strong connections with clients, uncover critical insights, and tailor your consulting approach to meet their specific needs. It allows you to better understand their challenges, build trust, and ultimately deliver more impactful solutions.

Concept 4: Mastering Effective Communication Techniques

Effective communication involves more than just listening. In this subsection, we'll delve into the techniques and strategies that will help you articulate your points clearly, adapt your communication style, and persuade others. Through real-life examples, we'll uncover the art of effective communication in negotiation.

Mastering Effective Communication Techniques refers to developing the skills and strategies necessary to communicate clearly, persuasively, and efficiently in a consulting context. As a consultant, effective communication is vital to building relationships, conveying ideas, influencing stakeholders, and achieving successful outcomes. Here's how you can get the most out of it:

Active Listening: Actively listening to your clients, colleagues, and stakeholders is essential for understanding their needs, concerns, and perspectives. Practice active listening by giving your full attention, asking clarifying questions, and demonstrating empathy. This will help you build rapport, gather relevant information, and establish trust.

Clarity and Conciseness: As a consultant, you often deal with complex concepts and information. Mastering the ability to communicate with clarity and conciseness is crucial. Use simple and jargon-free language, organize your thoughts coherently, and focus on delivering key messages. This will ensure your ideas are easily understood and remembered.

Nonverbal Communication: Nonverbal cues, such as body language, facial expressions, and tone of voice, play a significant role in effective communication. Be aware of your nonverbal signals and use them intentionally to convey confidence, sincerity, and openness. Pay attention to others' nonverbal cues as well, as they can provide valuable insights into their thoughts and feelings.

Adaptability: Different situations and stakeholders require different communication approaches. Being adaptable in your communication style allows you to connect with various individuals and adapt to their preferred communication methods. Tailor your communication to suit the needs of your audience, whether it's through written reports, presentations, or face-to-face discussions.

Feedback and Reflection: Actively seek feedback on your communication skills and reflect on your interactions. This feedback can come from colleagues, clients, or even recording and reviewing your own presentations. Pay attention to areas for improvement, such as clarity, engagement, or persuasive techniques, and make a conscious effort to refine your communication skills over time.

Technology Tools: Leverage technology tools that enhance communication effectiveness. Utilize presentation software, collaboration platforms, and video conferencing tools to communicate and collaborate seamlessly with your clients and team members. Stay updated with the latest communication tools and techniques to make the most of available technology.

By mastering effective communication techniques, you can build strong relationships, influence stakeholders, and effectively convey your expertise and ideas. This will enable you to have a greater impact as a consultant and contribute to the success of your clients' initiatives.

Concept 5: Building Relationships - The Bedrock of Successful Negotiations

Negotiations are not just about getting what you want; they're about building relationships that can lead to long-term success. In the world of consulting, relationships are the foundation on which successful negotiations are built. As a consultant, your ability to build strong and trust-based relationships with clients, stakeholders, and colleagues is crucial for achieving mutually beneficial outcomes. In this section, we will explore the key concepts, techniques, and tools to help you establish and nurture relationships that will enhance your negotiation skills.

Establishing Rapport and Trust: Building rapport and trust is the first step towards establishing a solid relationship. It starts with active listening and empathizing with the other party's needs and concerns. By showing genuine interest and understanding, you can create a positive atmosphere that encourages open communication and collaboration.

Developing a Win-Win Mindset: A win-win mindset is essential for building relationships based on mutual benefit. Rather than viewing negotiation as a zero-sum game, approach it with the belief that both parties can achieve their desired outcomes. This mindset fosters cooperation, problem-solving, and long-term partnerships.

Effective Communication and Influencing Skills: Strong communication skills are paramount in building relationships. Being able to articulate your ideas clearly, listen actively, and adapt your communication style to different individuals will help you connect with others on a deeper level. Additionally, developing influencing skills will enable you to effectively persuade and negotiate with stakeholders.

Emotional Intelligence and Relationship Management: Emotional intelligence plays a significant role in building relationships. Understanding and managing your emotions, as well as being attuned to the emotions of others, allows for better communication and conflict resolution. Developing emotional intelligence skills will help you navigate challenging situations and maintain positive relationships.

Networking and Relationship Building: Networking is a valuable tool for expanding your professional connections and building relationships. Attend industry events, join professional organizations, and engage in networking opportunities to meet potential clients and collaborators. Actively seek to build and nurture your network, as it can provide opportunities for future negotiations and referrals.

To maximize the benefits of building relationships in your consulting practice, consider the following tips:

Invest time in understanding your clients and stakeholders: Take the time to learn about their goals, priorities, and challenges. This understanding will enable you to tailor your negotiation strategies and propose solutions that align with their needs.

Be proactive in building and maintaining relationships: Initiate regular communication with clients and stakeholders, even outside of formal negotiation settings. Show genuine interest in their success and offer support where possible. This proactive approach will strengthen your relationships and increase the likelihood of successful negotiations.

Build a reputation as a trusted advisor: Consistently deliver high-quality work and demonstrate integrity in your interactions. Building a reputation as a trusted advisor will increase your credibility and influence in negotiations.

Continuously seek feedback and adapt: Request feedback from clients and stakeholders to understand their perception of your relationship-building efforts. Use this feedback to make improvements and adapt your approach as needed.

Remember, building relationships is an ongoing process that requires time, effort, and genuine care. By prioritizing relationship-building in your consulting practice, you will create a solid foundation for successful negotiations and foster long-term partnerships with your clients and stakeholders.

Concept 6: Finding Common Ground and Fostering Collaboration

Finding common ground involves identifying shared interests, goals, or values between parties involved in a negotiation. It allows you to establish a foundation of mutual understanding and build rapport, creating an atmosphere of cooperation rather than competition. As a consultant, finding common ground is essential because it helps in building trust and creating a collaborative environment with clients and stakeholders.

To get the most out of finding common ground, it's important to:

Conduct thorough research: Before entering into a negotiation, gather information about the other party's interests, needs, and priorities. This will help you identify potential areas of overlap and common ground.

Active listening and empathy: Listen attentively to the other party's perspective, concerns, and interests. Show empathy and try to understand their point of view. By doing so, you can find commonalities and demonstrate your willingness to collaborate.

Explore shared values and goals: Look for shared values or common objectives that both parties can align with. By emphasizing these shared aspects, you can foster a sense of collaboration and strengthen the likelihood of reaching a mutually beneficial agreement.

Seek win-win solutions: Focus on finding solutions that meet the interests of both parties. Look for creative options that address the needs and concerns of all stakeholders involved. By promoting win-win outcomes, you can foster collaboration and build strong working relationships.

Fostering collaboration involves creating an environment where all parties are actively engaged, contributing ideas, and working together towards a common goal. As a consultant, fostering collaboration is crucial as it allows you to harness the collective expertise and knowledge of your team and stakeholders, leading to more effective and innovative solutions.

To get the most out of fostering collaboration, consider the following:

Establish clear communication channels: Ensure that communication is open, transparent, and inclusive. Encourage active participation and create opportunities for everyone to share their ideas and perspectives.

Foster a culture of trust and respect: Create an environment where individuals feel safe to express their opinions and challenge ideas constructively. Encourage diversity of thought and value the contributions of all team members.

Facilitate effective teamwork: Encourage collaboration through teamwork and assign roles and responsibilities that promote cooperation and shared ownership of tasks. Encourage cross-functional collaboration to leverage different expertise and perspectives.

Use collaborative tools and techniques: Utilize tools and techniques such as brainstorming sessions, workshops, and collaborative software to facilitate idea generation and decision-making. These tools can enhance collaboration and encourage active participation.

By effectively finding common ground and fostering collaboration, consultants can build strong relationships with clients and stakeholders, achieve better outcomes, and create a positive and collaborative work environment.

Concept 7: Problem-Solving and Creative Solutions - Unleashing Your Innovative Thinking

Negotiation often requires creative problem-solving to find mutually beneficial solutions. In the world of consulting, problem-solving is a critical skill that can set you apart from others. As a consultant, your clients rely on you to tackle complex challenges and provide innovative solutions.

To solve a problem effectively, it's crucial to understand its nature and underlying causes. To do so, consider using brainstorming session to generate ideas, and techniques allowing you to evaluation options and make informed decisions. I believe we discussed at length already how to problem-solve and create solutions in Part 1. And, so, allow me this shortcut, and invite you to review Part 1 of this series.

Last but not least on this section, remember that problem-solving is rarely a one-time event. It often requires an iterative approach and continuous improvement. Thus, be patient, and willing to iterate. And if I may add one more thing: Problem-solving is not a solitary endeavor. Collaboration and building a problem-solving network are essential for success!

Remember, problem-solving is a mindset that can be cultivated and refined over time. Embrace challenges as opportunities for growth and creativity. Continuously seek out new perspectives, techniques, and approaches to expand your problem-solving repertoire.

Concept 8: Embracing a Problem-Solving Mindset

A problem-solving mindset is essential in negotiation. Embracing a Problem-Solving Mindset means approaching challenges and obstacles with a proactive and solution-oriented mindset. As a consultant, this mindset is crucial for effectively addressing client issues and delivering valuable solutions. Here's how you can get the most out of it:

Adopt a Growth Mindset: Embrace the belief that challenges are opportunities for growth and learning. View setbacks as stepping stones towards improvement and see each problem as a chance to develop new skills and knowledge.

Develop Analytical Thinking Skills: Enhance your ability to analyze complex problems by breaking them down into smaller, more manageable components. Use tools and frameworks such as root cause analysis, SWOT analysis, or fishbone diagrams to identify the underlying causes and potential solutions.

Foster Creativity and Innovation: Encourage creative thinking by exploring alternative approaches and considering out-of-the-box solutions. Embrace brainstorming sessions and encourage diverse perspectives to generate innovative ideas that can drive problem-solving.

Practice Systems Thinking: Recognize that problems are often interconnected and part of larger systems. Consider the broader implications and potential ripple effects of your proposed solutions. Take a holistic approach to problem-solving and consider the various stakeholders and factors involved.

Emphasize Collaboration: Engage in collaborative problem-solving by involving key stakeholders and subject matter experts. Foster open communication and create an environment that encourages sharing of ideas and perspectives. Leverage the collective intelligence of your team to arrive at the most effective solutions.

Utilize Data and Evidence: Make data-driven decisions by gathering and analyzing relevant information. Use data and evidence to support your proposed solutions and validate their potential effectiveness. Leverage technology and analytics tools to extract insights and make informed decisions.

Learn from Past Experiences: Reflect on past problem-solving experiences and extract valuable lessons. Analyze what worked well and what could have been done differently. Continuously improve your problem-solving approach based on feedback and outcomes.

By embracing a problem-solving mindset, you'll be better equipped to tackle complex challenges, find innovative solutions, and deliver exceptional results for your clients. It will set you apart as a consultant who can effectively navigate through obstacles and drive meaningful change.

Concept 9: Leveraging Creativity for Win-Win Solutions

Creativity is a powerful tool in negotiation. Leveraging creativity for win-win solutions is a key concept in advanced negotiation skills. It involves thinking outside the box, exploring innovative ideas, and finding mutually beneficial solutions that meet the interests of both parties involved in the negotiation.

As a consultant, getting the most out of leveraging creativity for win-win solutions requires a mindset shift. Here are some strategies to help you achieve this:

Embrace an open mindset: Be open to new perspectives and possibilities. Challenge conventional thinking and be willing to explore alternative options.

Foster a collaborative environment: Encourage open communication and collaboration with the other party. Create a safe space for sharing ideas and encourage brainstorming sessions.

Ask powerful questions: To stimulate creative thinking, ask thought-provoking questions that challenge assumptions and encourage innovative ideas. For example, "What if we approached this problem from a completely different angle?"

Break down silos: Break down silos within your own organization and collaborate across teams or departments. This cross-functional approach can bring together diverse expertise and lead to more creative solutions.

Use visual aids and storytelling: Incorporate visual aids, such as diagrams or infographics, to enhance your communication and make complex ideas more accessible. Additionally, storytelling can be a powerful tool to engage and inspire others during the negotiation process.

Encourage experimentation: Be open to experimenting with different ideas or approaches. Encourage the other party to do the same. This can help uncover innovative solutions that may not have been considered before.

Focus on interests, not positions: Look beyond the surface-level positions and identify the underlying interests of both parties. By understanding each party's motivations, you can find creative ways to address those interests and create win-win outcomes.

By embracing these strategies and cultivating a mindset of creativity, you can maximize your ability to find innovative solutions that satisfy the needs and interests of all parties involved. This will not only enhance your negotiation skills but also strengthen your reputation as a consultant who consistently delivers valuable and creative solutions to your clients.

Concept 10: Managing Difficult Situations - Navigating Challenges with Grace

Negotiations don't always go smoothly. There will be challenges, conflicts, and difficult situations along the way. As a consultant, you will inevitably encounter difficult situations and challenges during negotiations. How you handle these situations can make all the difference in the outcome. In this section, we will explore strategies for navigating challenges with grace and achieving positive results.

One key aspect of managing difficult situations is maintaining a calm and composed demeanor. When faced with conflict or resistance, it's important to stay level-headed and approach the situation with a problem-solving mindset. By keeping your emotions in check and staying focused on finding solutions, you can effectively navigate through challenging negotiations.

Another crucial aspect is active listening and effective communication. It's important to listen attentively to the concerns and perspectives of the other party involved. By showing empathy and understanding, you can build rapport and create an atmosphere of collaboration. Additionally, clear and concise communication is essential for conveying your own thoughts and proposals effectively.

Building on the concept of collaboration, finding common ground and seeking win-win solutions is vital. Instead of adopting a win-lose mentality, look for areas of shared interest and explore options that satisfy both parties' needs. This approach not only promotes cooperation but also enhances the likelihood of reaching mutually beneficial agreements.

Being adaptable and flexible is another key aspect of navigating challenges with grace. Sometimes, negotiations may take unexpected turns or encounter unforeseen obstacles. By embracing adaptability and being open to alternative solutions, you can adjust your approach and find creative ways to overcome obstacles and reach a favorable outcome.

Lastly, it's important to be prepared for difficult situations. Anticipate potential challenges, risks, and objections that may arise during negotiations. By doing thorough research and analysis beforehand, you can proactively address concerns and have well-thought-out responses. This level of preparedness will enhance your confidence and enable you to navigate difficult situations more effectively.

Remember, managing difficult situations with grace is not about avoiding conflict or suppressing your own needs. It's about finding the right balance between assertiveness and collaboration, maintaining a positive attitude, and focusing on achieving mutually beneficial outcomes. By mastering the art of managing difficult situations, you will strengthen your reputation as a skilled negotiator and consultant who can navigate challenges with grace and professionalism.

Concept 11: Managing Emotions and Maintaining Composure

Emotions can run high in negotiations, but maintaining composure is crucial. Managing Emotions and Maintaining Composure is a crucial aspect of advanced negotiation skills. It involves being aware of your own emotions, as well as effectively managing the emotions of others, during the negotiation process. As a consultant, mastering this skill is essential for maintaining professionalism, building rapport, and achieving successful outcomes in your engagements.

To get the most out of managing emotions and maintaining composure, consider the following strategies:

Self-awareness: Start by developing a strong sense of self-awareness. Understand your own triggers, emotions, and biases that may arise during negotiations. By recognizing your emotional state, you can better control and regulate your responses.

Emotional intelligence: Cultivate emotional intelligence, which involves being empathetic, understanding others' emotions, and effectively managing interpersonal dynamics. This skill allows you to respond appropriately to the emotions displayed by the other party, fostering a constructive and collaborative negotiation environment.

Stay calm under pressure: Negotiations can be intense and stressful, but it's important to stay calm and composed. Practice deep breathing techniques or other relaxation methods to manage stress and maintain a clear mind. This will help you think more clearly, make rational decisions, and communicate effectively.

Active listening: Actively listen to the other party's concerns, interests, and emotions. Show empathy and validate their perspective, even if you disagree. By demonstrating that you understand and respect their emotions, you can build trust and create a more positive negotiation environment.

Respond, don't react: Instead of reacting impulsively to emotional triggers, respond thoughtfully and strategically. Take a moment to pause, assess the situation, and choose your words and actions carefully. Responding rather than reacting allows you to maintain control and steer the negotiation towards a productive outcome.

Conflict resolution skills: Develop strong conflict resolution skills to effectively address and resolve any emotional conflicts that arise during negotiations. Focus on finding common ground, exploring alternative solutions, and seeking win-win outcomes.

Reflect and learn: After each negotiation, take time to reflect on your emotional responses and overall performance. Assess what worked well and what could be improved. Seek feedback from colleagues or mentors to gain insights into areas for growth. Continuous reflection and learning will help you refine your emotional management skills over time.

Remember, mastering the art of managing emotions and maintaining composure is an ongoing process. With practice and self-awareness, you can develop this skill and use it to your advantage in your consulting practice, leading to more successful negotiations and stronger client relationships.

Concept 12: Dealing with Difficult People and Resolving Conflicts

Difficult people and conflicts are inevitable in negotiation. Dealing with Difficult People and Resolving Conflicts is a crucial aspect of advanced negotiation skills for consultants. In this context, it refers to the ability to handle challenging personalities and navigate conflicts that may arise during negotiations. As a consultant, you will encounter a wide range of people with different communication styles, motivations, and approaches to problem-solving. It is essential to have strategies in place to effectively manage these situations and ensure productive outcomes.

To get the most out of dealing with difficult people and resolving conflicts as a consultant, consider the following:

Practice Active Listening: Actively listening to the other party's concerns and perspectives can help defuse tension and build rapport. Pay attention to their words, body language, and emotions to gain a deeper understanding of their underlying needs and motivations.

Maintain Emotional Intelligence: Emotional intelligence is key when dealing with difficult people. Keep your emotions in check and try to understand the emotions of others. Responding calmly and empathetically can help de-escalate conflicts and find common ground for resolution.

Find Common Interests and Shared Goals: Look for areas of agreement and shared objectives with the difficult person. By highlighting common interests, you can create a collaborative atmosphere and focus on finding win-win solutions.

Use Effective Communication Techniques: Clear and assertive communication is vital in resolving conflicts. Express your thoughts and concerns in a respectful manner, and encourage open and honest dialogue. Avoid confrontational language and personal attacks, as they can escalate tensions.

Collaborate and Problem-Solve: Engage in problem-solving discussions that involve brainstorming solutions and exploring alternatives together. Encourage the difficult person to contribute their ideas and perspectives. Collaborative problem-solving can lead to more sustainable and satisfactory resolutions.

Seek Mediation if Necessary: In situations where conflicts persist or become too challenging to handle independently, consider involving a neutral third party as a mediator. A mediator can help facilitate communication, clarify misunderstandings, and guide the negotiation process towards a resolution.

Remember, dealing with difficult people and resolving conflicts is a skill that requires practice and patience. By honing your abilities in this area, you can enhance your effectiveness as a consultant and build stronger relationships with clients and stakeholders.

Technique 1: BATNA (Best Alternative to a Negotiated Agreement) analysis

The BATNA analysis is a crucial technique in negotiation that involves identifying and assessing your best alternative if a negotiation does not result in a satisfactory agreement. As a consultant, mastering this technique will enable you to approach negotiations with a clear understanding of your alternatives and leverage them effectively.

To get the most out of the BATNA analysis as a consultant, follow these steps:

Identify your BATNA: Start by identifying and evaluating your best alternative to a negotiated agreement. This could be an alternative opportunity, a different negotiation partner, or even maintaining the status quo. Consider the potential outcomes, benefits, and risks associated with each alternative.

Assess the value and feasibility: Evaluate the value and feasibility of your BATNA. Consider factors such as the potential impact on your client's objectives, the resources required, and any dependencies or constraints. This assessment will help you determine the strength of your BATNA relative to the negotiation.

Use it strategically: Once you have a clear understanding of your BATNA, use it strategically during the negotiation process. Communicate your BATNA confidently to the other party when appropriate, as it can strengthen your position and increase your bargaining power. However, be cautious not to disclose too much information that may weaken your position.

Evaluate and reassess: Continuously evaluate and reassess your BATNA throughout the negotiation. As circumstances and dynamics change, your BATNA may evolve as well. Stay vigilant and adapt your strategy accordingly to maximize your advantage.

By effectively utilizing the BATNA analysis, you can negotiate from a position of strength, make informed decisions, and secure favorable outcomes for your clients. Remember, the key is to thoroughly analyze and understand your alternatives before entering into negotiations, ensuring that you are well-prepared and equipped to navigate the complexities of the negotiation process.

Technique 2: ZOPA (Zone of Possible Agreement) identification

The ZOPA, or Zone of Possible Agreement, is a key concept in negotiation that refers to the range of options where both parties can find common ground and reach an agreement. As a consultant, mastering the skill of identifying the ZOPA can greatly enhance your negotiation outcomes. Here's how you can get the most out of this technique:

Conduct thorough research and preparation: Before entering a negotiation, gather as much information as possible about the other party's needs, interests, and potential alternatives. This will help you identify the ZOPA and understand the potential areas of agreement.

Define your own interests and limits: Clearly define your own interests and priorities, as well as your walk-away point. This will help you assess the ZOPA and determine if the potential agreement aligns with your objectives.

Listen actively and ask probing questions: During the negotiation, listen attentively to the other party's concerns, needs, and proposed solutions. Ask probing questions to gain a deeper understanding of their perspective and identify potential areas of overlap.

Look for creative solutions: Sometimes, the ZOPA may not be immediately apparent. In such cases, use your creativity and problem-solving skills to explore alternative options that could expand the ZOPA and create mutually beneficial solutions.

Build rapport and trust: Establishing trust and rapport with the other party can help create a positive negotiation environment and increase the chances of finding common ground. Demonstrate empathy, respect, and openness throughout the negotiation process.

Maintain flexibility and be willing to compromise: Negotiation is a give-and-take process. Be flexible and willing to make concessions when it aligns with your overall objectives and the potential agreement falls within the ZOPA.

Keep the big picture in mind: While focusing on identifying the ZOPA, remember to keep the bigger picture in mind. Consider the long-term relationship with the other party and the potential impact of the agreement on your client's goals and objectives.

By effectively applying the ZOPA identification technique, you can uncover opportunities for mutual agreement and achieve optimal outcomes for your clients. It allows you to navigate the negotiation process with clarity, confidence, and the ability to find common ground even in complex situations.

Concept 13: Continuous Improvement - Mastering Negotiation Skills Over Time

Negotiation skills are not mastered overnight. It's a continuous learning process that requires dedication and practice. As a consultant, continuously improving your negotiation skills is essential for staying competitive and achieving successful outcomes for your clients. To get the most out of continuous improvement in negotiation skills, here are some key strategies to consider:

Seek feedback and reflect on experiences: Actively seek feedback from colleagues, clients, or mentors after each negotiation. Reflect on your performance, identify areas for improvement, and take action to address them. Embrace feedback as a valuable opportunity for growth and learning.

Engage in self-reflection and self-assessment: Regularly assess your own negotiation skills and identify areas where you excel and areas that need improvement. Take time to reflect on your negotiation style, strategies, and outcomes. Consider how you can leverage your strengths and address any weaknesses.

Stay updated on negotiation research and best practices: Keep yourself informed about the latest research, theories, and best practices in negotiation. Attend workshops, seminars, or training programs to stay up-to-date on new techniques and strategies. Incorporate new insights into your negotiation approach to enhance your effectiveness.

Practice and simulate negotiation scenarios: Actively practice your negotiation skills through role-plays, simulations, or mock negotiations. Create realistic scenarios that mimic the challenges you may encounter in your consulting engagements. By practicing in a safe environment, you can refine your techniques, experiment with different strategies, and build confidence.

Collaborate with peers and learn from others: Engage in discussions with fellow consultants or professionals who have expertise in negotiation. Share experiences, exchange insights, and learn from each other's successes and challenges. Collaborating with others can provide valuable perspectives and new ideas to incorporate into your own negotiation practice.

Analyze and learn from each negotiation experience: After every negotiation, take time to analyze the process and outcomes. Identify what worked well and what could have been done differently. Look for patterns, lessons learned, and strategies that led to successful outcomes. Continuously adapt and refine your approach based on your observations and insights.

Remember, continuous improvement in negotiation skills requires dedication, commitment, and a growth mindset. Embrace the journey of lifelong learning and development as you strive to become an exceptional negotiator in your consulting career.

Concept 14: Seeking Feedback and Reflecting on Experiences

Feedback is invaluable in improving your negotiation skills. Seeking feedback and reflecting on experiences is a crucial aspect of personal and professional growth as a consultant. It involves actively seeking input from others and critically analyzing your own performance to identify areas for improvement. Here's how you can get the most out of this practice:

Be open to feedback: Approach feedback with an open mind and a willingness to learn. Recognize that feedback is an opportunity for growth, even if it may be difficult to hear at times. Create a safe and supportive environment where colleagues, clients, and mentors feel comfortable providing honest feedback.

Seek feedback from diverse sources: Don't limit yourself to a single perspective. Seek feedback from a variety of sources, including clients, colleagues, supervisors, and even team members. Each perspective can offer valuable insights and help you gain a well-rounded understanding of your strengths and areas for improvement.

Ask specific questions: When seeking feedback, be specific about what you would like feedback on. For example, you can ask about your communication style, problem-solving approach, or leadership skills. This will guide the feedback provider and make the feedback more actionable.

Reflect on your experiences: Take time to reflect on your consulting experiences. Consider what went well, what could have been improved, and what lessons you learned from each project or interaction. Regularly journaling or maintaining a reflective practice can help you gain deeper insights and track your growth over time.

Identify patterns and themes: Look for patterns or recurring themes in the feedback you receive and the reflections you make. This will help you identify areas where you consistently excel and areas that need further development. Use this information to create a personalized development plan to address those areas.

Act on the feedback: Feedback without action is meaningless. Once you receive feedback and reflect on it, take steps to implement the suggested improvements. This may involve seeking additional training, seeking mentorship, or actively practicing new skills.

Continuously seek feedback: Seek feedback regularly, not just when you feel the need for improvement. Regular feedback allows you to stay on track and make incremental improvements over time. Foster a culture of feedback within your consulting practice, where everyone feels comfortable providing and receiving feedback.

By actively seeking feedback and reflecting on your experiences, you can uncover blind spots, enhance your self-awareness, and continuously improve your consulting skills. This practice will not only benefit you as a consultant but also contribute to better client relationships and successful engagements.

Concept 15: Practicing and Simulating Negotiation Scenarios

Practice makes perfect, and negotiation is no exception. Practicing and simulating negotiation scenarios is a crucial aspect of developing advanced negotiation skills as a consultant. It involves creating mock negotiation situations and actively participating in them to gain hands-on experience and refine your techniques. By immersing yourself in these simulated scenarios, you can effectively prepare for real-life negotiations and improve your overall negotiation effectiveness.

To get the most out of practicing and simulating negotiation scenarios as a consultant, consider the following tips:

Set clear objectives: Before starting a practice session, define your objectives for the negotiation. Identify the key issues, interests, and potential challenges you want to address. This will help you focus your practice and make it more meaningful.

Create realistic scenarios: Design negotiation scenarios that closely resemble the real-world situations you may encounter as a consultant. Consider factors such as industry dynamics, client expectations, and potential conflicts. The more realistic the scenarios, the more you can simulate the challenges and dynamics of actual negotiations.

Assume different roles: Assign different roles to yourself and other participants during the practice sessions. This will allow you to experience negotiations from various perspectives, such as that of a consultant, client, or stakeholder. Role-playing will enhance your understanding of different viewpoints and help you develop strategies to address diverse interests.

Seek feedback and reflect: After each simulated negotiation, seek feedback from your practice partners. Ask for their insights on your communication style, strategy, and overall performance. Reflect on what went well and areas for improvement. Incorporate the feedback into your future practice sessions to continuously refine your skills.

Analyze and debrief: Take time to analyze the outcomes of your practice negotiations. Assess the effectiveness of your strategies, techniques, and communication approaches. Identify patterns and trends that emerged during the simulations. Use these insights to adjust your approach and develop new strategies for future negotiations.

Practice active listening and observation: Pay close attention to verbal and non-verbal cues during the simulated negotiations. Practice active listening to understand the interests and concerns of the other party. Observe their body language, tone of voice, and overall demeanor to gain insights into their motivations and potential negotiation strategies. This will help you adapt your approach and effectively respond to their needs.

Embrace different negotiation styles: Experiment with different negotiation styles during your practice sessions. Try assertive, collaborative, and integrative approaches to understand their strengths and weaknesses. By being flexible and adapting your style to different situations, you can enhance your versatility as a negotiator.

Remember, practicing and simulating negotiation scenarios is an ongoing process. Dedicate regular time to honing your skills, seeking opportunities to practice with colleagues or mentors, and leveraging feedback to continually refine your approach. By investing in deliberate practice, you can enhance your ability to navigate complex negotiations and achieve favorable outcomes for both yourself and your clients.

Last, let me emphasize that negotiation is an art that evolves over time. Embrace every negotiation as an opportunity for growth, and continuously strive to improve your skills through practice and reflection. By mastering advanced negotiation skills, you'll not only achieve better outcomes for your clients but also strengthen your position as a trusted and influential consultant.

Practical Examples

To bring the concepts of advanced negotiation skills to life, let me present two examples of successful negotiations in consulting contexts.

Example 1: Negotiating a Contract Renewal

Let me share a personal experience where I had to utilize advanced negotiation skills to secure a contract renewal for my consulting services. I was working with a long-term client, and our existing contract was coming to an end. However, they had expressed interest in exploring other options and considering different consultants for their upcoming projects.

To ensure the continuation of our partnership, I recognized the need to demonstrate my value and negotiate favorable terms. I prepared extensively by analyzing our previous work, identifying the client's needs and pain points, and researching alternative solutions in the market. Armed with this knowledge, I entered the negotiation with confidence and a clear strategy.

During the negotiation, I emphasized the unique expertise and track record of success that my consulting firm brought to the table. I showcased the specific ways in which we had added value to their business in the past and presented innovative ideas for future projects. By highlighting our deep understanding of their industry and the benefits of maintaining a long-term partnership, I was able to sway their decision in our favor.

Through effective communication, active listening, and skilled persuasion, I successfully negotiated a contract renewal that not only met the client's needs but also secured favorable terms for my consulting firm. This experience showcased the significance of advanced negotiation skills in maintaining client relationships and securing business opportunities.

Example 2: Resolving Conflicts in a Multi-Stakeholder Project

In another instance, I found myself involved in a complex consulting project that involved multiple stakeholders with differing interests and priorities. As the project progressed, conflicts began to arise, threatening the overall progress and success of the initiative.

To navigate this challenging situation, I relied on advanced negotiation skills to facilitate productive discussions and find mutually beneficial solutions. I recognized the importance of fostering open communication and collaboration among the stakeholders to identify common ground and resolve conflicts effectively.

Using active listening techniques, I encouraged each stakeholder to express their concerns and perspectives. I then facilitated a series of negotiation sessions, where I helped the stakeholders explore their underlying interests, identify shared objectives, and find win-win solutions that addressed everyone's needs.

By employing principled negotiation techniques, I emphasized the importance of separating people from the problem and focusing on objective criteria. This approach allowed us to move beyond personal conflicts and work towards resolving the substantive issues at hand.

Through these negotiations, we were able to reach agreements on critical project decisions, reconcile conflicting interests, and restore collaboration among the stakeholders. This experience highlighted the power of advanced negotiation skills in managing complex projects and fostering effective stakeholder relationships.

These examples demonstrate how advanced negotiation skills enable consultants to navigate challenging situations, secure contract renewals, resolve conflicts, and achieve successful outcomes for both themselves and their clients. By mastering these skills, consultants can become skilled negotiators who can effectively advocate for their interests, build trust with stakeholders, and drive positive results.

Challenges and Common Mistakes to Avoid

Negotiations can be challenging and fraught with potential pitfalls. As a consultant, mastering the art of negotiation is crucial for achieving successful outcomes and building strong relationships with clients. However, it's important to be aware of the common challenges and pitfalls that can hinder your negotiation success. In this sub-chapter, I'll share personal stories and insights to help you navigate these challenges and avoid common mistakes in your consulting negotiations.

Challenge 1: Failing to Prepare Adequately

In the fast-paced world of consulting, it can be tempting to jump into negotiations without proper preparation. Let me share a story with you. I once had a high-stakes negotiation with a client, and I underestimated the time needed for preparation. As a result, I lacked a deep understanding of their needs and interests. It taught me the importance of investing time in thorough preparation to anticipate objections, identify potential areas of agreement, and gain a strategic advantage.

Challenge 2: Lack of Active Listening

Effective negotiation requires active listening skills, but it's easy to get caught up in making our own points and overlook the other party's perspective. I remember a negotiation where I was so focused on presenting my proposal that I failed to truly listen to the client's concerns. It led to misunderstandings and a breakdown in communication. Through this experience, I learned the value of active listening, which involves truly understanding the other party's interests, concerns, and underlying motivations.

Challenge 3: Being Overly Competitive

Competitiveness is a double-edged sword in negotiations. While it's essential to advocate for your interests, being overly competitive can harm relationships and hinder mutually beneficial agreements. I once found myself in a heated negotiation where I was determined to "win" at any cost. This mindset created tension and hindered collaboration. From that experience, I realized the importance of balancing assertiveness with cooperation to foster trust and achieve optimal outcomes.

Challenge 4: Neglecting Relationship Building

Building strong relationships with clients is key to successful negotiations, yet it's often overlooked. In one particular negotiation, I neglected to establish rapport with the client, and it resulted in a strained working relationship. Recognizing the significance of relationships, I now prioritize relationship building by taking the time to understand the other party's perspective, finding common ground, and fostering trust. This has helped me navigate negotiations more smoothly.

Challenge 5: Neglecting to Explore Interests

Focusing solely on positions can hinder negotiations. I recall a negotiation where both parties were fixated on their positions, resulting in a stalemate. It was only when we dug deeper to understand each other's underlying interests that we discovered mutually beneficial solutions. This experience taught me the importance of exploring interests, as they often hold the key to unlocking creative solutions that meet the needs of all parties involved.

Challenge 6: Failure to Manage Emotions

Emotions can run high during negotiations, and failing to manage them can lead to irrational decisions or escalated conflicts. I remember a negotiation where tensions flared, and emotions got the best of me. It was a valuable lesson in the need to stay composed and approach negotiations with a rational mindset. By managing emotions and remaining calm, I can better analyze the situation, make informed decisions, and maintain a constructive negotiation environment.

Challenge 7: Inflexibility and Lack of Creativity

In negotiations, being inflexible and resistant to exploring alternative solutions can limit your ability to reach mutually beneficial agreements. I once approached a negotiation with a rigid mindset, unwilling to consider alternative options. This approach led to a prolonged and unproductive negotiation. Since then, I've learned to embrace flexibility and creativity, allowing me to explore innovative solutions that address the interests of all parties involved.

Mastering advanced negotiation skills is an ongoing journey, filled with challenges and opportunities for growth. By being aware of these common challenges and mistakes, and drawing from personal experiences, you can navigate negotiations more effectively. Remember to invest time in preparation, actively listen to the other party, balance competitiveness with cooperation, build strong relationships, explore interests, manage emotions, and embrace flexibility and creativity. With practice and reflection, you'll become a skilled negotiator, driving successful outcomes in your consulting engagements.

Navigating these challenges and avoiding common mistakes requires continuous learning, self-awareness, and practice. By honing your negotiation skills, understanding the dynamics of each negotiation, and actively reflecting on your experiences, you can overcome these challenges and become a more effective negotiator in the world of consulting.

Exercises and Activities for Applying the Concepts

To reinforce your learning and provide opportunities for practical application, let's sharpen your negotiation skills through some exercises!

Exercise 1: Role-Play Scenarios

Create hypothetical negotiation scenarios that mimic real-life consulting situations. Assign different roles to yourself and a colleague or friend, and practice negotiating with each other. Focus on applying the concepts of active listening, exploring interests, and finding mutually beneficial solutions. Afterward, reflect on your performance and identify areas for improvement.

Exercise 2: Case Study Analysis

Select a real-life case study that involves a negotiation in the consulting field. Analyze the case study and identify the key negotiation strategies and techniques employed by the parties involved. Reflect on how you would approach the negotiation differently and what lessons you can learn from the case study. Discuss your findings with a colleague or mentor to gain additional insights.

Exercise 3: Mindful Negotiation Journal

Keep a journal where you document your negotiation experiences in consulting engagements. Reflect on each negotiation, noting the challenges you faced, the strategies you employed, and the outcomes achieved. Use this journal as a tool for self-reflection and improvement. Regularly review your entries to identify patterns, strengths, and areas where you can further develop your negotiation skills.

Remember, practice is key to honing your advanced negotiation skills. By engaging in these exercises and activities, you'll gain valuable experience and insight that will enhance your abilities as a consultant.

Conclusion

"The most successful negotiations are those where everyone walks away feeling like they've won." – Unknown

In conclusion, the chapter on advanced negotiation skills has explored the crucial role that negotiation plays in a consultant's daily work life. We have examined key concepts such as active listening, exploring interests, finding mutually beneficial solutions, and managing emotions. These skills are essential for consultants to navigate complex situations, build relationships, and achieve favorable outcomes.

We have discussed various techniques and tools, including preparation and planning, creating value, understanding power dynamics, and managing difficult conversations. By applying these strategies, consultants can enhance their negotiation effectiveness and create win-win solutions for themselves and their clients.

Additionally, we have highlighted the importance of practicing and simulating negotiation scenarios to develop and refine skills. By engaging in role-plays, analyzing case studies, and maintaining a mindful negotiation journal, consultants can continuously improve their negotiation abilities and gain valuable experience.

Furthermore, we have examined common challenges and mistakes to avoid, such as overconfidence, neglecting active listening, failing to understand the other party's interests, and letting emotions cloud judgment. By being aware of these challenges, consultants can navigate negotiations more effectively and achieve better outcomes.

To end this chapter, let me simply say that mastering advanced negotiation skills is essential for consultants to excel in their roles. By understanding the key concepts, employing effective techniques and tools, and avoiding common mistakes, consultants can negotiate with confidence, build strong client relationships, and achieve successful outcomes in their consulting engagements.

As we move forward, the next chapter will delve into another critical skill: emotional intelligence. We will explore how emotional intelligence impacts consulting interactions, the key components of emotional intelligence, and practical strategies for developing and leveraging this skill to enhance consulting effectiveness.

Chapter 14: Emotional Intelligence for Consulting

Picture this—I was in the middle of a high-stakes client meeting, discussing a critical project that had hit a roadblock. Tensions were running high, and the atmosphere was thick with frustration. As the consultant leading the discussion, I could feel the weight of the situation on my shoulders. I knew that the success of this project hinged not only on technical expertise but also on the ability to navigate complex emotions and build strong relationships.

In that moment, I realized the immense power of emotional intelligence in the world of consulting. It's not just about being smart and knowledgeable; it's about understanding and managing emotions—both our own and those of others. It's about recognizing that people make decisions based on their feelings and perceptions, and being able to connect with them on a deeper level.

As consultants, we are not just problem solvers and subject matter experts; we are also relationship builders and influencers. Our ability to understand, manage, and leverage emotions can have a profound impact on our interactions with clients, colleagues, and stakeholders. Emotional intelligence allows us to navigate complex dynamics, communicate effectively, build trust, and ultimately make a lasting impact.

Hence, in this chapter, we will embark on a journey to explore the key principles, concepts, and strategies of emotional intelligence that are crucial for your consulting practice. But before we dive into the depths of emotional intelligence, let's take a moment to reflect on why it is so vital for consultants like us. Emotional intelligence allows us to connect on a deeper level, understand the needs and motivations of our clients, and build strong relationships based on trust and empathy. It enables us to navigate conflicts, adapt to changing circumstances, and influence stakeholders effectively. By mastering emotional intelligence, we can enhance our consulting effectiveness and make a lasting impact.

So, buckle up, because the world of emotional intelligence is waiting to be discovered.

Introduction to the Emotional Intelligence for Consulting

In this chapter, we will explore the importance of emotional intelligence for consultants and how it can significantly impact your effectiveness in consulting engagements. Emotional intelligence for consulting refers to the ability of a consultant to understand, manage, and leverage emotions in their work. It encompasses a set of skills and qualities that enable consultants to navigate complex interpersonal dynamics, communicate effectively, build trust, and influence others.

For a consultant, emotional intelligence means being aware of one's own emotions and how they impact their thoughts and actions. It also involves understanding and empathizing with the emotions of others, including clients, colleagues, and stakeholders. By developing emotional intelligence, consultants can better navigate challenging situations, build strong relationships, and make informed decisions that consider both rational and emotional factors.

Emotional intelligence allows consultants to adapt to different personalities, manage conflicts, and handle high-pressure situations with grace and composure. It helps them build rapport with clients, understand their needs and motivations, and tailor their approach accordingly. Consultants with high emotional intelligence are skilled in reading nonverbal cues, managing their own emotions under stress, and effectively communicating their ideas and recommendations.

In a nutshell, emotional intelligence is a crucial aspect of a consultant's toolkit. It helps them build and maintain successful relationships, influence stakeholders, and ultimately deliver exceptional value to their clients. By mastering emotional intelligence, consultants can elevate their consulting practice and drive positive outcomes in their engagements.

Key Concepts, Techniques, and Tools

How many times did I stand outside the meeting room, my heart pounding in my chest? I can't tell you. But what I can tell you is that it's always about doing a critical client presentation. I remember this time when I needed to make a strong impression. As I took a deep breath to calm my nerves, I couldn't help but think about the importance of emotional intelligence in consulting.

Emotional intelligence, or EQ, is a crucial skill set that goes beyond technical expertise. It involves understanding and managing our own emotions and effectively relating to others. In the world of consulting, where relationships and communication are key, emotional intelligence plays a vital role in our success.

Concept 1: Self-Awareness - The Power of Knowing Yourself

To be effective consultants, we must first understand ourselves. Self-awareness is the foundation of emotional intelligence. It involves recognizing and understanding our own emotions, strengths, weaknesses, and triggers.

Techniques such as self-reflection, mindfulness, and seeking feedback from trusted colleagues can help us gain deeper insights into our emotions and behaviors. By being aware of our own reactions and patterns, we can better manage our emotions and make conscious choices in our consulting interactions.

Self-awareness is the key to understanding ourselves and our emotions, and it forms the foundation of emotional intelligence. As consultants, self-awareness allows us to recognize our strengths, weaknesses, and triggers, enabling us to manage our emotions and make conscious choices in our interactions. Here's how to get the most out of self-awareness as a consultant:

Practice self-reflection: Set aside time regularly to reflect on your thoughts, emotions, and reactions in various consulting situations. Ask yourself questions like, "How did I handle that client meeting?" or "What emotions did I experience during that challenging conversation?" Reflecting on these experiences helps you gain insights into your patterns of behavior and emotional responses.

Seek feedback: Reach out to trusted colleagues, mentors, or supervisors and ask for their honest feedback on your strengths and areas for improvement. They may offer valuable perspectives and help you identify blind spots you may not be aware of.

Develop mindfulness: Mindfulness involves being fully present in the moment and non-judgmentally observing your thoughts, emotions, and bodily sensations. Engaging in mindfulness practices such as meditation or breathing exercises can help you become more attuned to your emotions and reactions in real-time.

Keep a journal: Maintaining a journal can be a powerful tool for self-awareness. Write down your thoughts, emotions, and experiences in consulting engagements. This practice allows you to track patterns, identify triggers, and gain deeper insights into your emotional landscape.

Embrace continuous learning: Stay open to learning and self-improvement. Seek out resources such as books, articles, or workshops that delve into self-awareness and emotional intelligence. Engage in professional development opportunities that help you understand yourself better and enhance your consulting skills.

By actively cultivating self-awareness, you can gain a deeper understanding of yourself as a consultant, manage your emotions effectively, and make conscious choices that contribute to your success in consulting engagements.

Concept 2: Self-Regulation - Mastering Emotional Control

In the fast-paced world of consulting, emotions can run high. The ability to regulate and control our emotions is crucial. By practicing self-regulation, we can manage our impulses, remain composed, and respond thoughtfully in high-pressure situations.

Techniques like deep breathing, reframing negative thoughts, and practicing emotional self-control enable us to navigate challenging moments with grace and composure. By mastering self-regulation, we can maintain our professionalism and effectively handle even the most difficult client conversations.

Self-regulation, or mastering emotional control, is a key concept in emotional intelligence that refers to the ability to manage and control one's emotions in different situations. As a consultant, self-regulation is crucial for maintaining composure, professionalism, and making sound decisions even in high-pressure and challenging circumstances.

To get the most out of self-regulation as a consultant, here are some techniques and strategies to consider:

Recognize your triggers: Take time to identify the situations or events that tend to evoke strong emotional responses in you. By understanding your triggers, you can be better prepared to manage your emotions when faced with those triggers.

Practice self-awareness: Develop a strong sense of self-awareness by regularly reflecting on your emotions, thoughts, and reactions. Take note of any patterns or recurring emotional responses you may have and consider how they impact your interactions with clients and colleagues.

Develop emotional self-control techniques: Explore various techniques that help you regulate your emotions. Deep breathing exercises, mindfulness, and meditation can be effective in calming your mind and creating space for thoughtful responses rather than impulsive reactions.

Reframe negative thoughts: Challenge negative thoughts or interpretations that may fuel strong emotional reactions. Replace negative self-talk with more positive and constructive thoughts to maintain a balanced perspective in challenging situations.

Seek support and feedback: Engage with mentors, coaches, or trusted colleagues who can provide feedback and support in managing your emotions. Their insights and guidance can help you gain new perspectives and develop strategies for emotional control.

Practice empathy: Cultivate empathy for others, as it can help you develop a more compassionate and understanding approach in your interactions. By considering the perspectives and emotions of others, you can navigate difficult conversations more effectively and build stronger relationships.

Prioritize self-care: Taking care of your physical and mental well-being is essential for maintaining emotional balance. Prioritize activities that help you relax, recharge, and manage stress. Engage in hobbies, exercise regularly, and practice self-care rituals to support your emotional well-being.

Remember, self-regulation is a skill that takes time and practice to develop. By consistently applying these techniques and strategies, you can enhance your ability to master emotional control and become a more effective and resilient consultant.

Concept 3: Empathy - The Art of Understanding Others

Empathy is a powerful tool for consultants. It involves putting ourselves in others' shoes, understanding their emotions, and showing genuine care and compassion. By practicing active listening, seeking to understand before being understood, and demonstrating empathy, we can build trust and rapport with our clients.

Empathy is a fundamental aspect of emotional intelligence that plays a vital role in the consulting profession. It is the ability to understand and share the feelings of others, putting ourselves in their shoes and seeing the world from their perspective. As a consultant, developing empathy allows us to connect with our clients on a deeper level, understand their needs and concerns, and provide more meaningful and tailored solutions.

To get the most out of empathy as a consultant, here are some key strategies and techniques:

Active Listening: Actively listen to your clients, paying close attention to their words, tone of voice, and body language. Show genuine interest and curiosity in understanding their thoughts and feelings. Avoid interrupting and practice reflective listening by summarizing and paraphrasing what they've said to ensure you've understood correctly.

Perspective-Taking: Put yourself in the client's position and try to see things from their point of view. Consider their background, experiences, and challenges they may be facing. This helps you develop a more comprehensive understanding of their needs and concerns.

Ask Open-Ended Questions: Use open-ended questions to encourage clients to express themselves more fully. This allows them to share their thoughts and emotions, giving you deeper insights into their needs and expectations. Avoid asking leading questions or jumping to conclusions.

Non-Verbal Communication: Pay attention to non-verbal cues such as facial expressions, body language, and tone of voice. These can provide valuable information about the client's emotions and help you better understand their perspective. Be mindful of your own non-verbal communication as well, as it can impact how the client perceives your empathy.

Empathetic Language: Use language that demonstrates empathy and understanding. Show validation and empathy by acknowledging and reflecting back the client's emotions. For example, you can say, "I can understand how frustrating that must be for you" or "It sounds like you're feeling overwhelmed, and I'm here to support you."

Cultivate Curiosity and Open-Mindedness: Approach each client interaction with curiosity and an open mind. Suspend judgment and be willing to explore different viewpoints. This helps create a safe and supportive space where clients feel comfortable sharing their thoughts and emotions.

Practice Empathy in Team Interactions: Empathy is not limited to client interactions. It is equally important in collaborating with colleagues and stakeholders. Practice empathy within your team by understanding their perspectives, appreciating their strengths, and supporting their challenges. This fosters a positive and collaborative work environment.

By cultivating empathy as a consultant, you can deepen your understanding of clients, build stronger relationships, and deliver more impactful solutions. Empathy allows you to tailor your approach, communicate effectively, and ultimately provide value that meets the unique needs of each client.

Concept 4: Relationship Management - Building Strong Connections

Consulting is a people-centric profession, and building strong relationships is essential. Effective relationship management involves effective communication, conflict resolution, collaboration, and building trust through authenticity and integrity.

Relationship Management - Building Strong Connections is a key concept in emotional intelligence for consultants. It involves effectively managing and nurturing relationships with clients, colleagues, and stakeholders to foster trust, collaboration, and mutual success.

As a consultant, building strong connections is essential for long-term success. Here are some strategies to get the most out of relationship management:

Communication: Effective communication is the cornerstone of relationship management. It is important to actively listen, understand the needs and concerns of others, and communicate clearly and transparently. Regular and open communication builds trust and helps to align expectations.

Trust and Integrity: Trust is the foundation of any successful relationship. As a consultant, it is crucial to demonstrate integrity, honesty, and reliability. By consistently delivering on commitments and maintaining confidentiality, you can earn and maintain the trust of your clients and colleagues.

Collaboration: Collaboration is key to building strong connections. Actively seek opportunities to collaborate with clients and colleagues, leveraging their expertise and insights. Encourage a collaborative and inclusive approach, valuing diverse perspectives and fostering a sense of teamwork.

Emotional Intelligence: Emotional intelligence plays a significant role in relationship management. Being aware of your own emotions and managing them effectively helps you respond empathetically to others. Show empathy, respect, and understanding towards the emotions and needs of your clients and colleagues.

Conflict Resolution: Conflict is inevitable in any working relationship. As a consultant, develop skills in conflict resolution to address conflicts effectively and constructively. Act as a mediator and find win-win solutions that satisfy the interests of all parties involved.

Networking: Networking is a powerful tool for relationship management. Actively participate in industry events, conferences, and professional associations to expand your network. Build relationships with key individuals who can support your consulting journey and provide valuable insights and opportunities.

Continual Engagement: Building strong connections requires ongoing engagement. Stay connected with your clients and colleagues beyond the project scope. Regularly check in, provide updates, and offer assistance when needed. Nurture relationships by showing genuine interest and support.

By focusing on relationship management and applying these strategies, you can foster strong connections that lead to successful consulting engagements, repeat business, and positive referrals. Remember, strong relationships are built on trust, effective communication, collaboration, and mutual respect. By understanding and applying emotional intelligence in our relationships with clients, colleagues, and stakeholders, we can foster a positive and productive consulting environment.

Concept 5: Social Awareness - Reading the Room

In a group or team setting, social awareness is crucial. It involves observing and understanding the emotions and needs of others. By reading non-verbal cues, observing group dynamics, and adapting our communication style, we can effectively connect with different individuals and create an inclusive and collaborative consulting environment.

Social Awareness - Reading the Room is the ability to observe and understand the emotions, dynamics, and unspoken cues in a group or team setting. As a consultant, being socially aware allows you to navigate interpersonal relationships, adapt your communication style, and effectively collaborate with others. Here's how you can get the most out of it:

Pay attention to non-verbal cues: Observe the body language, facial expressions, and tone of voice of those around you. These non-verbal cues can provide valuable insights into people's emotions and attitudes.

Listen actively: Practice active listening by focusing on what others are saying and demonstrating genuine interest in their perspectives. This will help you understand their emotions and needs better.

Seek diverse perspectives: Be open to different viewpoints and actively engage with individuals from various backgrounds and experiences. This will broaden your understanding of different emotions and perspectives within a group.

Adapt your communication style: Tailor your communication approach to suit the needs and preferences of those you're interacting with. This may involve adjusting your tone, using appropriate language, or finding common ground to build rapport.

Show empathy and understanding: Demonstrate empathy by acknowledging and validating the emotions of others. This can create a sense of trust and connection, leading to more productive and collaborative interactions.

Manage conflicts effectively: When conflicts arise, strive to understand the underlying emotions and interests of all parties involved. By addressing conflicts with empathy and respect, you can find mutually beneficial solutions and maintain positive relationships.

Stay attuned to group dynamics: Observe how individuals interact with each other and how the group functions as a whole. This awareness will help you navigate power dynamics, identify potential challenges, and foster a more inclusive and harmonious work environment.

By developing social awareness and actively reading the room, you can enhance your ability to understand and connect with others. This will enable you to build stronger relationships, navigate complex group dynamics, and contribute effectively to your consulting engagements.

Concept 6: Emotional Agility - Navigating Complex Situations

Consulting often involves navigating complex and uncertain situations. Emotional agility is the ability to adapt and respond to different emotional circumstances with flexibility and resilience. By recognizing and managing our emotions in the face of challenges, embracing change, and staying focused, we can thrive in the dynamic consulting landscape.

Emotional agility is the ability to adapt and respond to different emotional circumstances with flexibility and resilience. As a consultant, you will encounter complex situations that require you to navigate diverse emotions and effectively manage your responses. Here's how you can get the most out of emotional agility:

Recognize and acknowledge your emotions: Take the time to understand and identify your emotions in challenging situations. This self-awareness will help you gain clarity on how you are feeling and how it may impact your decision-making and interactions.

Practice mindfulness: Cultivate the practice of being present in the moment and observing your thoughts and emotions without judgment. Mindfulness can help you create space to pause, reflect, and respond thoughtfully rather than react impulsively.

Foster a growth mindset: Embrace the belief that challenges are opportunities for growth and learning. Instead of being overwhelmed by complex situations, view them as a chance to develop new skills, broaden your perspectives, and find innovative solutions.

Build resilience: Develop your resilience by adopting coping strategies that help you bounce back from setbacks and maintain a positive mindset. This might include seeking support from colleagues or mentors, engaging in self-care activities, and practicing self-compassion.

Embrace change and uncertainty: In the consulting world, change and uncertainty are constants. Develop the ability to adapt to new circumstances and embrace the unknown. This flexibility will allow you to navigate complex situations with confidence and adapt your approach as needed.

Seek diverse perspectives: When facing complex situations, seek input from others and value diverse perspectives. This can help you gain a broader understanding of the situation, consider alternative viewpoints, and make more informed decisions.

Reflect and learn from experiences: After navigating a complex situation, take the time to reflect on the outcomes and lessons learned. Consider what worked well and what could have been improved. This reflection will help you continuously grow and enhance your emotional agility.

Remember, emotional agility is a skill that can be developed with practice and intentional effort. By honing your ability to navigate complex situations with flexibility and resilience, you will be better equipped to handle the challenges and uncertainties that arise in your consulting career.

Concept 7: Tools and Techniques - Enhancing Emotional Intelligence

As consultants, emotional intelligence is a crucial aspect of our work. By developing and applying these key concepts, techniques, and tools, we can enhance our emotional intelligence, leading to more effective communication, stronger relationships, and greater success in our consulting engagements.

Various tools and techniques can support the development of emotional intelligence. These may include journaling, self-assessment questionnaires, emotional intelligence training programs, and coaching or mentoring relationships. By utilizing these resources, we can continue to refine and strengthen our emotional intelligence skills.

Developing and enhancing emotional intelligence requires intentional effort and practice. In this section, we will explore some tools and techniques that can help consultants enhance their emotional intelligence skills and get the most out of their consulting practice.

Journaling: Keeping a journal can be a powerful tool for self-reflection and self-awareness. Take a few minutes each day to reflect on your emotions, thoughts, and experiences. Write down any insights or patterns you notice. Journaling can help you gain a deeper understanding of yourself and your emotional reactions, allowing you to make conscious choices in your consulting interactions.

Self-Assessment Questionnaires: There are various self-assessment questionnaires available that can provide insights into your emotional intelligence strengths and areas for development. Examples include the Emotional Intelligence Appraisal, the Mayer-Salovey-Caruso Emotional Intelligence Test (MSCEIT), and the Emotional Competence Inventory (ECI). Taking these assessments can help you identify specific areas to focus on and guide your personal development efforts.

Emotional Intelligence Training Programs: Consider enrolling in emotional intelligence training programs or workshops. These programs provide a structured approach to learning and developing emotional intelligence skills. They often include activities, exercises, and discussions that help participants understand and apply emotional intelligence principles in real-life scenarios. Look for programs that offer practical techniques and strategies that you can directly apply to your consulting practice.

Coaching or Mentoring Relationships: Engaging in coaching or mentoring relationships can be incredibly valuable for enhancing your emotional intelligence. A coach or mentor can provide guidance, support, and feedback as you navigate emotional challenges and develop your skills. They can help you identify blind spots, offer alternative perspectives, and provide strategies for improving your emotional intelligence in specific contexts.

To get the most out of these tools and techniques as a consultant, it's important to approach them with an open mind and a willingness to learn and grow. Here are some tips to maximize their effectiveness:

Set aside dedicated time for self-reflection and practice. Consistency is key when developing emotional intelligence skills.

Be honest with yourself and embrace self-awareness. Recognize your strengths and areas for improvement without judgment.

Actively apply what you learn in real-life situations. Look for opportunities to practice emotional intelligence in your consulting interactions.

Seek feedback from others. Ask for input from trusted colleagues, mentors, or clients to gain different perspectives and insights on your emotional intelligence.

Stay committed to your personal development journey. Emotional intelligence is a lifelong skill, and continuous practice and growth are necessary for ongoing improvement.

By utilizing these tools and techniques and approaching them with dedication and openness, you can enhance your emotional intelligence and become a more effective and successful consultant. And, naturally, by understanding and applying these key concepts, techniques, and tools, consultants can enhance their emotional intelligence, leading to more effective communication, stronger relationships, and greater success in their consulting engagements.

Practical Examples

To illustrate the application of emotional intelligence in a consulting context, this section presents a couple of real-life scenarios that highlight how emotional intelligence can influence client interactions, team dynamics, and overall project success.

Example 1: Managing Client Expectations

I was working with a client who had high expectations for a project's outcome within a tight timeline. The client's pressure and demands were causing stress and tension among the team members. I realized the importance of applying emotional intelligence to manage this challenging situation effectively.

Using self-awareness, I recognized my own emotions and the impact I had on my interactions with the client and team members. I remained calm and composed, avoiding reacting impulsively to the client's demands. I then employed empathy to understand the client's underlying concerns and pressures. By actively listening and asking open-ended questions, I was able to gain a deeper understanding of the client's perspective and expectations.

With emotional intelligence, I used effective communication to manage expectations. I set realistic goals, clearly communicated project timelines, and negotiated mutually agreed-upon deliverables with the client. I also involved the team in the conversation, ensuring everyone's input and concerns were considered.

As a result, the client felt heard and understood, and the team members felt supported and valued. The project proceeded smoothly, and my emotional intelligence skills played a crucial role in fostering positive relationships and achieving successful outcomes.

Example 2: Conflict Resolution

During a consulting engagement, I encountered a conflict between team members from different departments. The conflicting parties had opposing views on a project's approach, leading to communication breakdowns and decreased collaboration.

Applying emotional intelligence, I recognized the importance of managing emotions and facilitating effective dialogue to resolve the conflict. I actively listened to each person's perspective, demonstrating (at least I tried as much as I could) empathy and understanding for their concerns.

I then I facilitated a constructive conversation where team members felt safe to express their opinions and emotions. I encouraged open dialogue and guided the group towards finding common ground and a mutually beneficial solution. By employing emotional intelligence techniques, such as active listening, perspective-taking, and collaboration, I believe I did help the team members see the value in each other's viewpoints. Through this process, I fostered a sense of unity and alignment among the team, enabling them to move forward with a shared vision and increased productivity.

These real-world examples demonstrate how agile emotional intelligence can positively impact consulting engagements by promoting effective communication, managing conflicts, and building strong relationships. By leveraging emotional intelligence skills, you too can navigate complex situations, foster collaboration, and achieve successful outcomes.

Challenges and Common Mistakes to Avoid

As a consultant, you understand the importance of emotional intelligence in building successful client relationships and driving project outcomes. However, it's essential to be aware of the challenges and common mistakes that can hinder the application of emotional intelligence in the consulting world. In this chapter, we will explore these challenges and share practical insights to help you navigate them effectively.

While emotional intelligence can be a powerful asset, there are also challenges and common mistakes to be aware of and avoid. In this section, we' talk about some of these challenges.

Challenge 1: Lack of Self-Awareness

Picture this: I was working on a high-pressure project, juggling multiple deadlines, and barely taking time for myself. I realized that I had become so consumed with work that I neglected my own emotions. This lack of self-awareness was impacting my ability to effectively manage my emotions and understand their impact on others.

To overcome this challenge, I started incorporating regular self-reflection into my routine. Taking a few moments each day to check in with myself and acknowledge my emotions helped me develop greater self-awareness. It enabled me to recognize triggers and patterns, allowing me to respond more thoughtfully in challenging situations.

Challenge 2: Difficulty Empathizing with Clients and Colleagues

During a client meeting, I noticed a clash of opinions and emotions between team members. It was clear that some struggled to understand and empathize with each other's perspectives. This lack of empathy was hindering effective collaboration and putting the project at risk.

I realized the importance of actively practicing empathy. By making a conscious effort to listen attentively, ask open-ended questions, and validate others' experiences, I fostered a deeper understanding of their emotions and perspectives. This enabled me to build stronger relationships, bridge differences, and facilitate productive conversations.

Challenge 3: Ineffective Communication

I recall a situation where a miscommunication between a client and our team caused unnecessary confusion and delays. Upon reflection, I realized that ineffective communication, influenced by emotions, played a significant role in the breakdown.

I recognized the need to improve my communication skills by incorporating emotional intelligence techniques. This included active listening, being mindful of non-verbal cues, and expressing my thoughts and emotions assertively and empathetically. By focusing on effective communication, I was able to foster better understanding, build trust, and navigate conflicts more constructively.

Challenge 4: Difficulty Managing Conflict

In a high-stakes project, tensions rose between team members due to conflicting opinions and tight deadlines. The inability to manage conflict effectively was hindering progress and straining relationships.

I learned to approach conflicts with a calm and composed demeanor, actively listening to all parties involved and seeking to understand their perspectives. By encouraging open dialogue, finding common ground, and fostering a collaborative problem-solving approach, I was able to resolve conflicts more effectively and maintain a positive team dynamic.

Challenge 5: Ignoring Emotional Intelligence in Decision-Making

I recall a project where decisions were made solely based on logical analysis, ignoring the emotional aspects and human factors involved. This led to missed opportunities and strained client relationships.

Recognizing the importance of emotional intelligence in decision-making, I started considering the emotional impact and human dynamics alongside the logical aspects. By involving stakeholders, actively seeking their input, and taking into account their emotions and needs, I made more well-rounded decisions that fostered trust and alignment.

Mastering emotional intelligence in the consulting world is an ongoing journey, but being aware of the challenges and common mistakes is a crucial step. By navigating the challenges of self-awareness, empathizing with others, improving communication, managing conflicts effectively, and incorporating emotional intelligence into decision-making, you can enhance your consulting practice. Embracing emotional intelligence will not only strengthen your relationships with clients and colleagues but also drive better project outcomes and pave the way for long-term success in the consulting field.

By being aware of these challenges and common mistakes, consultants can proactively work towards enhancing their emotional intelligence skills. Practicing self-awareness, empathy, effective communication, conflict resolution, and incorporating emotional intelligence into decision-making can lead to improved client relationships, better collaboration, and ultimately, greater success in consulting engagements.

Exercises and Activities for Applying the Concepts

Here are two exercises that can help you apply the concepts of emotional intelligence in your consulting daily practice:

Exercise 1: Self-Reflection Journaling

Set aside a few minutes each day to reflect on your emotions, reactions, and interactions throughout the day. Write down any situations where you felt a strong emotional response and analyze the underlying triggers and patterns. Consider how you could have responded differently and more effectively. This exercise will enhance your self-awareness and help you identify areas for growth in emotional intelligence.

Exercise 2: Empathy Mapping Exercise

Choose a client or colleague with whom you have regular interactions. Take some time to put yourself in their shoes and try to understand their perspective, needs, and emotions. Create an empathy map by drawing a quadrant and labeling each section as "Thinking," "Feeling," "Seeing," and "Doing." Fill in each section with observations and insights about their thoughts, emotions, observations, and actions. This exercise will enhance your empathy skills and enable you to better connect with and understand others.

Exercise 3: Conflict Resolution Role Play

Enlist a colleague or friend to engage in a role-play scenario where you simulate a conflict situation that could arise in your consulting work. Practice active listening, assertive communication, and finding common ground to reach a resolution. Reflect on the experience afterward and identify areas for improvement in managing conflicts effectively.

These exercises will help you apply the concepts of emotional intelligence in practical ways and enhance your skills as a consultant. Remember to approach them with an open mind and a willingness to learn and grow.

Conclusion

"Emotional intelligence is a skill that can transform the way we approach our work and relationships, enabling us to create positive and impactful change." – Unknown

In conclusion, the chapter on emotional intelligence for consulting has explored the importance of emotional intelligence in the consulting world and provided valuable insights and tools to enhance this essential skill set. Here are the key points discussed:

Understanding Emotional Intelligence: Emotional intelligence is the ability to recognize and understand emotions in oneself and others, and to use this awareness to manage emotions effectively. It plays a crucial role in building strong relationships, communicating effectively, and navigating complex situations.

The Benefits of Emotional Intelligence: Developing emotional intelligence has numerous benefits for consultants, including improved communication, better client relationships, enhanced leadership skills, and increased resilience and adaptability in challenging situations.

Key Concepts and Techniques: The chapter introduced key concepts such as self-awareness, self-regulation, empathy, and social skills. It also provided techniques and tools for enhancing emotional intelligence, including self-reflection, active listening, emotional regulation strategies, and empathy-building exercises.

Challenges and Mistakes to Avoid: The chapter highlighted common challenges and mistakes when applying emotional intelligence, such as letting emotions cloud judgment, neglecting self-care, and failing to recognize the emotions of others. It emphasized the importance of practicing self-awareness and continuously striving for growth.

Exercises and Activities: To apply the concepts of emotional intelligence in daily consulting practice, the chapter suggested exercises such as self-reflection journaling, empathy mapping, and conflict resolution role plays. These activities help consultants strengthen their self-awareness, empathy, and communication skills.

Developing emotional intelligence is an ongoing journey that requires self-reflection, practice, and continuous learning. By mastering emotional intelligence, consultants can navigate complex situations, build strong relationships, and make a positive impact in their consulting work.

Chapter 15: Conflict Resolution and Management

Picture this: You walk into a meeting room filled with tense energy. As a consultant, you have been called in to help resolve a long-standing conflict between two teams in a client organization. The room is buzzing with frustration, misunderstandings, and a palpable sense of discord. Your heart beats a little faster as you prepare to tackle this challenging situation head-on.

Today, here and now, I want to take you on a journey to explore the fascinating world of conflict resolution and management. It's a skill that can make or break a consultant, and it's one that I've learned the hard way. In this chapter, we will dive into the complexities of conflict, understanding its root causes, and exploring effective strategies to manage and resolve it. We'll uncover the key concepts, techniques, and tools that can help you navigate through difficult conversations, bridge divides, and find solutions that satisfy all parties involved.

But before we delve into the strategies and techniques, let me share a story that shaped my perspective on conflict resolution.

A few years ago, I was working on a project for a client where two department heads, let's call them John and Sarah, were constantly at odds. Their disagreements had become toxic, affecting team morale and impeding progress on the project. It was a classic case of conflicting egos and misaligned goals.

In my initial meeting with both parties, I could sense their hostility and distrust towards each other. It was clear that if this conflict wasn't addressed, the project would suffer greatly. I knew I had to find a way to bring them together and find common ground.

Throughout the weeks that followed, I utilized various conflict resolution techniques. We facilitated open and honest dialogue, encouraging each party to express their concerns and frustrations. We worked on building empathy and understanding by encouraging active listening and perspective-taking. We also introduced a collaborative problem-solving approach that focused on shared goals and finding win-win solutions.

It wasn't an easy process. There were heated arguments, moments of frustration, and setbacks along the way. But through persistent effort and a commitment to finding common ground, we were able to help John and Sarah develop a newfound understanding and appreciation for each other's perspectives. They began to communicate more effectively, collaborate, and make decisions that benefited both teams and the project as a whole.

This experience taught me the power of conflict resolution and management in the consulting world. It's not just about resolving conflicts; it's about transforming them into opportunities for growth, innovation, and stronger relationships.

In the upcoming sections, we will explore the key concepts, techniques, and tools that will equip you to handle conflicts like a seasoned consultant. We'll discuss active listening, effective communication, negotiation skills, mediation, and more. We'll also delve into the common challenges and mistakes to avoid, as well as provide practical exercises and activities to help you hone your conflict resolution skills.

So, let's dive in and discover the art of conflict resolution and management in the odd world of consulting.

Introduction to Conflict Resolution and Management

Conflict resolution and management is the process of addressing and resolving conflicts or disagreements that arise within a professional setting. In the context of consulting, conflict resolution and management refer to the ability to effectively handle and navigate conflicts that may arise between team members, stakeholders, or clients.

As a consultant, conflict resolution and management are crucial skills to possess because conflicts can hinder progress, damage relationships, and impede the successful completion of projects. By understanding and applying conflict resolution techniques, consultants can address conflicts in a constructive manner, fostering collaboration, understanding, and ultimately reaching mutually beneficial resolutions.

In the consulting practice, conflict resolution and management involve actively listening to all parties involved, understanding their perspectives, and facilitating open and respectful communication. It requires the ability to identify the underlying causes of conflicts, such as differing goals, communication breakdowns, or personality clashes, and finding ways to address these root issues.

Consultants skilled in conflict resolution and management are adept at using negotiation, mediation, and problem-solving techniques to bridge gaps, build consensus, and reach mutually satisfactory outcomes. They understand the importance of maintaining professionalism, managing emotions, and building trust to navigate through conflicts effectively.

By mastering conflict resolution and management, consultants can not only resolve conflicts but also turn them into opportunities for growth, innovation, and strengthened relationships. It allows consultants to facilitate productive discussions, maintain positive working environments, and achieve successful outcomes for their clients and teams.

Key Concepts, Techniques, and Tools

Imagine this: you're on a stormy sea, sailing through uncharted waters as a consultant. Suddenly, you encounter a conflict, a clash of interests and perspectives. As the waves crash around you, it's essential to steer through the turmoil with finesse. Well, in this chapter, we will explore the art of conflict resolution and management, equipping you with the tools to navigate these stormy seas and emerge stronger.

Concept 1: Active Listening - Riding the Waves of Understanding

As I reflect on my journey as a consultant, I recall a time when I encountered a heated debate between team members. The tension was palpable, and it seemed impossible to find common ground. However, I realized the importance of active listening. By truly hearing each person's concerns and perspectives, I was able to navigate the waves of misunderstanding and guide the team towards a resolution.

As a consultant, one of the most valuable skills you can possess is the art of active listening. Active listening goes beyond simply hearing what others are saying – it involves fully engaging with them, understanding their perspectives, and building rapport. When you master this skill, you can navigate the waves of understanding, fostering meaningful connections and resolving conflicts more effectively.

To get the most out of active listening as a consultant, consider the following techniques:

Give your full attention: When engaging in a conversation, dedicate your full attention to the person speaking. Put aside distractions and show genuine interest in what they are saying. Maintain eye contact and use non-verbal cues to signal your attentiveness.

Practice empathy: Empathy is the ability to understand and share the feelings of another person. Put yourself in the shoes of your clients, colleagues, or team members. Seek to understand their perspectives, challenges, and emotions. This empathetic approach will help you establish rapport and build trust.

Ask open-ended questions: Encourage open and meaningful dialogue by asking open-ended questions. These questions invite others to share their thoughts and feelings, providing deeper insights into their perspectives. Avoid yes/no questions and instead, ask questions that begin with "what," "how," or "tell me about."

Reflect and paraphrase: Show that you are actively listening by reflecting and paraphrasing what the speaker has said. Summarize their key points or rephrase their statements to ensure you have understood them correctly. This not only demonstrates your attentiveness but also allows for clarification and validation.

Practice non-judgment: Keep an open mind and suspend judgment when engaging in conversations. Avoid jumping to conclusions or forming opinions prematurely. By creating a safe space for open dialogue, you encourage others to express themselves freely, leading to a deeper understanding of their perspectives.

Practice active body language: Your body language can convey your engagement and receptiveness. Maintain an open posture, lean in slightly, and nod your head to show that you are actively listening. Use facial expressions to demonstrate empathy and understanding.

Avoid interruptions: Interrupting others can derail the flow of conversation and hinder effective communication. Practice patience and wait for the speaker to finish before offering your thoughts or responses. This shows respect for their perspective and allows for a more productive exchange.

Take notes: Consider taking notes during conversations to capture important points, concerns, or ideas. This not only helps you remember the details but also shows that you value what the speaker is saying.

By incorporating these techniques into your consulting practice, you can enhance your ability to actively listen and ride the waves of understanding. Active listening fosters better communication, builds trust, and allows for more effective conflict resolution. Ultimately, it enables you to serve your clients better and achieve successful outcomes in your consulting engagements.

Concept 2: Effective Communication - Clearing the Fog of Conflict

Another memory comes to mind: a client meeting where miscommunication threatened to derail our progress. In that moment, I understood the power of effective communication. By articulating our ideas clearly and encouraging open dialogue, we were able to clear the fog of conflict and find a way forward that satisfied everyone involved.

Effective communication is a crucial component of conflict resolution and management in the consulting world. It involves the clear and concise exchange of ideas, thoughts, and information to ensure that everyone involved understands each other's perspectives and needs. As a consultant, mastering effective communication can help you clear the fog of conflict and create an atmosphere conducive to resolution. Here's how you can get the most out of it:

Active Listening: Actively listen to all parties involved in the conflict. Give them your full attention, maintain eye contact, and show genuine interest in understanding their viewpoints. Avoid interrupting and make sure to clarify any points of confusion. By actively listening, you demonstrate respect and create a foundation for effective communication.

Clarity and Conciseness: When expressing your thoughts and ideas, be clear and concise. Use simple and straightforward language, avoiding jargon or technical terms that may confuse others. Structure your message in a logical manner and focus on the key points to ensure that your message is easily understood by all parties involved.

Open and Honest Communication: Foster an environment of open and honest communication. Encourage all individuals to express their concerns, needs, and perspectives without fear of judgment or reprisal. Create a safe space where everyone feels comfortable sharing their thoughts and emotions. By promoting open dialogue, you can uncover underlying issues and work towards finding common ground.

Nonverbal Communication: Pay attention to nonverbal cues such as body language, facial expressions, and tone of voice. These cues can provide valuable insights into the emotions and intentions of others. Be mindful of your own nonverbal communication, ensuring that it aligns with your verbal message and conveys openness and receptiveness.

Feedback and Clarification: Throughout the communication process, provide feedback and seek clarification. Repeat key points to ensure understanding and ask questions to gain deeper insights. Offer constructive feedback when necessary, focusing on the behavior or issue at hand rather than attacking the individual. By seeking and providing feedback, you can improve mutual understanding and resolve conflicts more effectively.

Adaptability: Recognize that different individuals have different communication styles. Be adaptable and adjust your communication approach to suit the preferences and needs of others. Some individuals may prefer more direct and assertive communication, while others may respond better to a more empathetic and collaborative approach. Adapting your communication style can foster better understanding and collaboration.

Document and Follow-Up: After discussions and agreements are made, document the key points and decisions to ensure clarity and avoid any misunderstandings. Follow up with all parties involved to ensure that the agreed-upon actions are being implemented and that any remaining concerns or issues are addressed promptly.

By honing your skills in effective communication, you can clear the fog of conflict and create an environment where conflicts can be resolved in a constructive and collaborative manner.

Concept 3: Emotional Intelligence - Anchoring Stability in Troubled Waters

During a particularly challenging engagement, I realized the impact of emotional intelligence. As emotions ran high, I learned to regulate my own emotions and empathize with the feelings of others. This anchor of stability allowed me to navigate through the stormy seas of conflict with grace and compassion, fostering an environment conducive to resolution.

Emotional intelligence is the ability to understand and manage your own emotions, as well as recognize and empathize with the emotions of others. As a consultant, emotional intelligence plays a crucial role in navigating conflicts and resolving them effectively. It allows you to anchor stability in troubled waters and foster an environment conducive to resolution. Here's how you can get the most out of emotional intelligence as a consultant:

Self-Awareness: Start by developing self-awareness, which involves recognizing and understanding your own emotions, triggers, and biases. Reflect on your emotional responses in different situations, particularly during conflicts. This awareness will help you regulate your emotions and maintain composure when faced with challenging circumstances.

Empathy: Cultivate empathy, the ability to understand and share the feelings of others. Put yourself in the shoes of those involved in the conflict and try to understand their perspectives and underlying motivations. By demonstrating empathy, you can build trust and rapport, creating a safe space for open communication and conflict resolution.

Active Listening: Practice active listening, which involves fully engaging and understanding the messages being conveyed by others. Listen not just to the words spoken, but also to the emotions and concerns behind them. Pay attention to non-verbal cues and validate the emotions expressed by acknowledging and empathizing with them. This level of attentive listening will help create an atmosphere of understanding and support.

Emotional Regulation: Learn to regulate your own emotions during conflicts. Stay calm and composed, even in the face of intense emotions. Take a step back and breathe deeply before responding, allowing yourself time to process and choose your words carefully. By managing your emotions effectively, you can avoid escalating conflicts and find rational and constructive solutions.

Conflict Resolution Skills: Develop skills in conflict resolution, such as active problem-solving, negotiation, and mediation. These skills will allow you to approach conflicts with a level-headed mindset, seeking win-win solutions and finding common ground. Apply your emotional intelligence to create an atmosphere of collaboration and cooperation, focusing on shared interests rather than personal agendas.

Continuous Learning: Embrace a mindset of continuous learning and improvement in emotional intelligence. Seek feedback from colleagues, mentors, or coaches to gain insights into how your emotions and communication style impact your interactions during conflicts. Actively seek out resources, workshops, or training programs to further develop your emotional intelligence skills.

By incorporating emotional intelligence into your consulting practice, you can anchor stability in troubled waters. It enables you to navigate conflicts with empathy, understanding, and effective communication, ultimately leading to successful resolution and strengthened client relationships.

Concept 4: Negotiation and Mediation - Charting a Course for Win-Win Solutions

A vivid memory surfaces: a client project where conflicting interests threatened to derail progress. Through negotiation and mediation techniques, I facilitated discussions that focused on interests rather than positions. By exploring various options and finding compromises, we charted a course towards win-win solutions that satisfied the needs of all parties involved.

In the world of consulting, negotiation and mediation skills are essential for charting a course towards win-win solutions. As a consultant, you often find yourself in situations where conflicting interests and differing viewpoints need to be reconciled. Whether it's resolving conflicts within a team or facilitating discussions between clients and stakeholders, your ability to negotiate and mediate effectively can make all the difference.

Negotiation involves the process of reaching an agreement by finding common ground and compromise. It requires careful preparation, active listening, and the ability to navigate complex dynamics. As a consultant, getting the most out of negotiation means:

Understanding Interests and Positions: Rather than focusing solely on positions, it's important to dig deeper and identify the underlying interests of all parties involved. By understanding what drives each side, you can uncover areas of potential agreement and craft win-win solutions that meet everyone's needs.

Preparing Strategically: Before entering a negotiation, take the time to prepare strategically. Clarify your own objectives and desired outcomes, anticipate the interests and concerns of the other party, and develop a range of options for potential agreements. This preparation will give you confidence and flexibility during the negotiation process.

Active Listening and Effective Communication: During negotiations, practice active listening to truly understand the perspectives and concerns of the other party. This allows you to build rapport, demonstrate empathy, and create an environment of trust. Effective communication skills, such as clear articulation of your own interests and the ability to ask open-ended questions, are also crucial in ensuring that all parties are heard and understood.

Seeking Win-Win Solutions: The goal of negotiation should be to seek win-win solutions where both parties feel satisfied with the outcome. Look for creative solutions that address the interests of all parties involved and explore options that expand the pie rather than dividing it. By fostering a collaborative mindset and a focus on mutual gains, you can reach agreements that leave everyone feeling like winners.

Mediation, on the other hand, involves facilitating discussions and guiding parties towards a mutually acceptable resolution. As a consultant, mediation skills can be invaluable when dealing with conflicts among team members, clients, or stakeholders. To make the most out of mediation, consider the following:

Maintaining Neutrality and Impartiality: As a mediator, it is crucial to remain neutral and impartial. Your role is to facilitate the conversation, encourage open dialogue, and help parties find common ground. By staying unbiased and avoiding taking sides, you can create an environment where trust can flourish.

Building Rapport and Establishing Trust: Building rapport with all parties involved is essential in mediation. Create a safe and respectful space for dialogue, actively listen to each party's perspective, and demonstrate empathy. Establishing trust is crucial for parties to feel comfortable sharing their concerns and working towards a resolution.

Managing Emotions and Diffusing Tension: Conflicts often come with heightened emotions and tensions. As a mediator, it is important to manage these emotions and diffuse tension effectively. Encourage parties to express their emotions while maintaining a calm and neutral demeanor. By acknowledging and validating emotions, you can help parties move past their differences and focus on finding common ground.

Facilitating Constructive Communication: Your role as a mediator is to facilitate constructive communication between parties. Encourage active listening, help parties reframe their perspectives, and guide them towards productive dialogue. By creating an atmosphere of respect and understanding, you can guide the discussion towards a resolution that meets everyone's interests.

In summary, negotiation and mediation skills are essential for consultants in navigating conflicts and facilitating resolution. By understanding interests, preparing strategically, practicing active listening, seeking win-win solutions, maintaining neutrality, building rapport, managing emotions, and facilitating constructive communication, you can maximize the potential for positive outcomes in your consulting engagements.

Concept 5: Problem-Solving - Discovering Hidden Treasures amidst Conflict

In one particularly complex engagement, conflict seemed insurmountable. However, by applying problem-solving skills, we identified the underlying issues causing the conflict and unearthed hidden opportunities for resolution. Through analytical thinking and creative brainstorming, we navigated the stormy waters and emerged with innovative solutions that surpassed our initial expectations.

As a consultant, problem-solving is an essential skill when it comes to resolving conflicts and finding mutually beneficial solutions. It involves a structured approach to identifying, analyzing, and solving complex problems that arise during consulting engagements. Problem-solving is like embarking on a treasure hunt amidst the stormy waters of conflict, where the gems of resolution and innovation lie hidden. To get the most out of problem-solving as a consultant, follow these key steps:

Define the problem: Begin by clearly defining the problem at hand. What is the underlying issue causing the conflict? Understand the interests and perspectives of all parties involved. This step lays the foundation for effective problem-solving.

Gather information: Dive deep into the problem by gathering relevant information. Conduct research, interview stakeholders, and collect data to gain a comprehensive understanding of the situation. The more information you have, the better equipped you'll be to uncover hidden insights and potential solutions.

Analyze the problem: Break down the problem into its components and analyze each part separately. Use tools like root cause analysis, SWOT analysis, or fishbone diagrams to identify the underlying causes and contributing factors. This analytical approach will help you unravel the complexity of the conflict and identify potential areas for resolution.

Generate alternative solutions: Encourage creative thinking and brainstorm multiple alternative solutions. Encourage input from all stakeholders involved in the conflict. This step is about exploring possibilities and generating a range of ideas without judgment. Remember, sometimes the most innovative solutions emerge from unexpected sources.

Evaluate and select the best solution: Evaluate the pros and cons of each alternative solution against the interests and objectives of all parties involved. Consider feasibility, potential risks, and the impact on relationships. Select the solution that aligns best with the desired outcomes and has the highest likelihood of success.

Implement and monitor progress: Once a solution is chosen, develop a clear plan for implementation. Assign responsibilities, set milestones, and establish a monitoring mechanism to track progress. Regularly assess the effectiveness of the solution and make adjustments as necessary.

Learn from the process: Reflect on the problem-solving process and the outcomes achieved. Identify lessons learned and areas for improvement. By continually refining your problem-solving skills, you'll become more adept at discovering hidden treasures amidst conflict in future engagements.

To get the most out of problem-solving as a consultant, foster a collaborative and inclusive environment. Encourage open communication and actively involve all stakeholders in the process. Embrace diversity of thought and create space for innovative ideas to emerge. Remember, problem-solving is not just about finding a solution, but also about building relationships, promoting trust, and fostering a culture of continuous improvement.

By mastering the art of problem-solving, you will navigate the stormy seas of conflict with confidence and uncover the hidden treasures of resolution and innovation.

Concept 6: Collaboration and Consensus-Building - Sailing as One Team

In a challenging cross-functional project, I learned the value of collaboration and consensus-building. By fostering a sense of shared responsibility and encouraging open communication, we transformed conflicting perspectives into a unified vision. Sailing as one team, we steered our ship towards success, leaving behind the stormy seas of discord.

As a consultant, you often find yourself working with diverse teams and stakeholders, each with their own ideas and perspectives. Collaboration and consensus-building are essential skills that enable you to harness the collective intelligence and creativity of the team. It is about creating an environment where everyone feels heard, valued, and included, ultimately leading to stronger and more impactful outcomes.

To get the most out of collaboration and consensus-building as a consultant, consider the following:

Foster a Culture of Trust and Respect: Build trust within the team by demonstrating integrity, transparency, and accountability. Encourage open and respectful communication, where everyone feels safe to express their opinions and ideas. Embrace diversity and value different perspectives, as this will enrich the team's collective knowledge and problem-solving capabilities.

Define Clear Goals and Expectations: Set clear goals and objectives for the team to align their efforts towards a common purpose. Ensure that everyone understands the desired outcomes and the specific roles and responsibilities of each team member. By establishing clear expectations, you can minimize misunderstandings and conflicts along the way.

Promote Active Participation and Collaboration: Create opportunities for active participation and collaboration among team members. Encourage brainstorming sessions, workshops, and group discussions where everyone can contribute their ideas and insights. Use facilitation techniques to ensure equal participation and create a space where everyone's voice is heard and valued.

Foster a Consensus-Driven Approach: Consensus-building is about reaching agreement or common ground among team members. It does not necessarily mean that everyone will fully agree with every decision, but rather finding a solution that everyone can support and commit to. Encourage open dialogue, active listening, and constructive feedback to reach consensus effectively. Be open to compromise and find win-win solutions that address the interests of all parties involved.

Leverage Conflict Constructively: Conflict can arise during the collaboration process, and it is important to view it as an opportunity for growth and innovation rather than a barrier. Embrace healthy debate and encourage constructive conflict resolution. Provide a platform for discussing and addressing conflicts openly, allowing for different perspectives to be heard and reconciled. By addressing conflicts early on, you can prevent them from escalating and hindering progress.

Effective Communication and Documentation: Clear and effective communication is crucial for successful collaboration. Ensure that information is shared in a timely and transparent manner, and that everyone is kept informed of progress and decisions. Document important discussions, agreements, and action items to maintain clarity and accountability throughout the collaboration process.

Celebrate Success and Learn from Challenges: Acknowledge and celebrate the achievements and milestones reached through collaboration. Recognize the efforts and contributions of team members, fostering a sense of accomplishment and motivation. Additionally, learn from challenges and setbacks encountered along the way. Reflect on what worked well and identify areas for improvement to enhance future collaboration endeavors.

By embracing collaboration and consensus-building as a consultant, you can harness the collective wisdom and strengths of the team, leading to more innovative and impactful solutions. Sailing as one team, you can navigate through the stormy waters of conflict and complexity, achieving shared goals and delivering exceptional results.

Concept 7: Emotional Regulation - Finding Calm in the Midst of Chaos

In the midst of a high-pressure engagement, I encountered moments of intense conflict. However, by mastering emotional regulation, I remained calm and composed. By navigating my own emotional reactions and creating a positive atmosphere, I guided others to find common ground and navigate through the stormy waves of disagreement.

As a consultant, you are often faced with high-pressure situations, tight deadlines, and conflicting interests. In the midst of this chaos, it is essential to master the art of emotional regulation. Emotional regulation refers to the ability to manage and control your own emotions, maintaining a sense of calm and composure even in challenging circumstances. By developing this skill, you can navigate conflicts with greater clarity and effectiveness.

To get the most out of emotional regulation as a consultant, consider the following techniques and strategies:

Self-awareness: Start by cultivating self-awareness of your own emotions. Pay attention to how you feel in different situations and understand how your emotions can influence your thoughts and actions. Recognize when you are experiencing stress, frustration, or anger, and be mindful of how these emotions may impact your decision-making and interactions with others.

Breathwork and relaxation techniques: When faced with a stressful situation or conflict, take a moment to focus on your breath. Deep breathing exercises can help activate your body's relaxation response, calming your mind and reducing the intensity of negative emotions. Incorporate relaxation techniques such as meditation, mindfulness, or yoga into your daily routine to build resilience and emotional stability.

Pause and reflect: In the heat of the moment, it can be tempting to react impulsively. However, practicing emotional regulation involves taking a step back and pausing before responding. Use this moment of pause to reflect on the situation, consider the consequences of different actions, and choose a response that aligns with your long-term goals and values.

Empathy and perspective-taking: Developing empathy towards others involved in the conflict can help you regulate your own emotions. Try to understand their perspective and consider the factors that may be contributing to their emotions and behavior. This empathetic understanding can foster a more compassionate and constructive approach to conflict resolution.

Seek support and self-care: As a consultant, it's crucial to prioritize self-care and seek support when needed. Take breaks, engage in activities that bring you joy and relaxation, and connect with a supportive network of colleagues, friends, or mentors. Surrounding yourself with positive influences and seeking guidance when faced with challenging situations can help you maintain emotional balance and resilience.

Reflect and learn from experiences: After resolving a conflict or navigating a challenging situation, take the time to reflect on the experience. Consider what strategies worked well and what could be improved. This reflective practice allows you to learn from each encounter, continuously refine your emotional regulation skills, and develop a deeper understanding of yourself and others.

By mastering emotional regulation, you can bring a sense of calm and stability to your consulting practice. This skill will not only enhance your own well-being but also enable you to approach conflicts with a clear mind, better communicate with stakeholders, and build stronger relationships. Remember, emotional regulation is a lifelong journey, and with practice and perseverance, you can become a master of finding calm in the midst of chaos.

Concept 8: Cultural Sensitivity - Navigating Multicultural Waters

In a global project, cultural differences threatened to create tumultuous waters. However, by embracing cultural sensitivity, I recognized and respected diverse perspectives. Understanding how culture can impact conflict dynamics and communication styles, I steered our ship through these multicultural waters with empathy and inclusivity.

As a consultant, you'll often find yourself working in diverse and multicultural environments. These waters can be both enriching and challenging, requiring a keen sense of cultural sensitivity. Navigating these multicultural waters means understanding and respecting different cultural norms, values, and communication styles. It means embracing diversity and leveraging it as a source of strength rather than a hindrance. Here's how you can get the most out of cultural sensitivity as a consultant:

Embrace Diversity: Recognize that diversity brings a wealth of perspectives and experiences to the table. Embrace this diversity and see it as an opportunity to learn, grow, and gain new insights. Appreciate the unique perspectives that individuals from different cultures can offer and be open to incorporating them into your work.

Develop Cultural Awareness: Take the time to educate yourself about different cultures. Learn about their customs, traditions, and communication styles. This knowledge will help you navigate cultural differences with sensitivity and respect. It will also enable you to adapt your approach and communication to be more effective in cross-cultural settings.

Practice Empathy and Respect: Cultivate empathy and respect towards individuals from different cultures. Put yourself in their shoes and try to understand their point of view. Be mindful of any biases or assumptions you may have and approach interactions with an open mind and genuine curiosity. Treat everyone with respect, regardless of their cultural background.

Adapt Communication Styles: Communication can vary greatly across cultures. Be flexible in your communication approach and adapt it to suit the cultural context. Pay attention to non-verbal cues, such as body language and tone of voice, as they can carry significant meaning. Strive to communicate clearly and concisely, avoiding jargon or language that may be difficult for others to understand.

Build Relationships: Building strong relationships is key to successful consulting engagements. Invest time in building rapport and trust with individuals from different cultures. Show genuine interest in their backgrounds and perspectives. Building strong relationships will help bridge cultural gaps and facilitate effective collaboration.

Seek Feedback: Regularly seek feedback from colleagues and clients from different cultures. Ask for their perspective on your communication style, approach, and any areas where you can improve your cultural sensitivity. Actively listen to their feedback and make adjustments as necessary. This continuous learning process will help you refine your cultural sensitivity skills over time.

Foster Inclusivity: Create an inclusive environment where everyone feels valued and respected, regardless of their cultural background. Encourage diverse perspectives and ensure that everyone has a voice in decision-making processes. Foster a culture of inclusivity and actively work towards breaking down cultural barriers and biases.

By practicing cultural sensitivity, you can navigate the multicultural waters of consulting with grace and effectiveness. Embrace diversity, develop cultural awareness, practice empathy and respect, adapt communication styles, build relationships, seek feedback, and foster inclusivity. These practices will not only enhance your ability to work successfully in diverse environments but also contribute to building stronger relationships and achieving better outcomes in your consulting engagements.

Concept 9: Conflict Management Tools - Equipping the Voyage

Throughout my consulting journey, I have relied on various conflict management tools. From conflict resolution frameworks to decision-making matrices, these tools have served as my navigational aids, guiding me through the treacherous waters of conflict resolution with clarity and purpose.

As a consultant, conflicts are an inevitable part of your journey. To effectively navigate these turbulent waters, it is crucial to have a set of conflict management tools at your disposal. These tools provide structure, guidance, and clarity in resolving conflicts and reaching mutually beneficial outcomes. Let's explore some key conflict management tools and how to get the most out of them in your consulting practice.

Conflict Resolution Frameworks: Various conflict resolution frameworks, such as the Thomas-Kilmann Conflict Mode Instrument or the Interest-Based Relational Approach, provide a systematic approach to understanding and addressing conflicts. Familiarize yourself with these frameworks, understand their underlying principles, and apply them to different conflict scenarios. By using a structured approach, you can better analyze the conflict, identify underlying issues, and generate potential solutions.

Decision-Making Matrices: In complex conflicts where multiple options are available, decision-making matrices can be invaluable. These matrices help evaluate and prioritize different solutions based on specific criteria or factors. Create decision-making matrices tailored to your project or client's needs, considering factors like feasibility, impact, and alignment with strategic objectives. By objectively assessing potential solutions, you can make informed decisions that lead to optimal outcomes.

Facilitation Techniques: Facilitation techniques play a vital role in managing conflicts during meetings or group discussions. Techniques such as active listening, brainstorming, and consensus-building can help create a supportive environment where all parties feel heard and respected. Develop your facilitation skills by practicing these techniques and adapting them to different conflict situations. By fostering open dialogue and encouraging collaboration, you can guide the group towards a mutually agreeable resolution.

Communication Tools: Effective communication is at the heart of conflict management. Utilize communication tools like nonviolent communication, paraphrasing, and assertiveness to express your thoughts and understand the perspectives of others. Practice active listening and empathy to ensure that all parties feel understood and valued. By mastering these communication tools, you can foster constructive dialogue, diffuse tensions, and build rapport with conflicting parties.

Negotiation Strategies: Negotiation is a critical skill in conflict resolution. Familiarize yourself with negotiation strategies such as principled negotiation or integrative bargaining. Understand the importance of win-win outcomes and seek creative solutions that address the interests of all parties involved. Develop your negotiation skills by engaging in role-playing exercises or participating in negotiation simulations. By honing your negotiation strategies, you can navigate conflicts more effectively and reach mutually beneficial agreements.

Emotional Intelligence: Emotional intelligence plays a significant role in conflict management. Enhance your self-awareness, self-regulation, empathy, and social skills to better navigate emotional dynamics during conflicts. Practice emotional regulation techniques like deep breathing, mindfulness, and reframing to remain calm and composed in challenging situations. By cultivating emotional intelligence, you can defuse conflicts, build trust, and foster positive relationships with clients, colleagues, and stakeholders.

To get the most out of these conflict management tools, integrate them into your consulting practice deliberately. Continuously enhance your knowledge and understanding of these tools through books, workshops, or online courses. Actively seek opportunities to apply them in real-life consulting scenarios, whether through client projects or internal team dynamics. Reflect on your experiences, learn from each conflict resolution process, and refine your approach accordingly.

Remember, mastering conflict management tools takes time and practice. Embrace each conflict as a learning opportunity and remain open to feedback and continuous improvement. By equipping yourself with these tools and utilizing them effectively, you can transform conflicts into opportunities for growth, collaboration, and successful consulting engagements.

As a consultant, conflict is inevitable. However, by honing your skills in conflict resolution and management, you can navigate these stormy seas with confidence and grace. Remember the power of active listening, effective communication, emotional intelligence, negotiation and mediation, problem-solving, collaboration, emotional regulation, cultural sensitivity, and the tools at your disposal. With these tools in your arsenal, you can weather any storm, forging a path towards resolution and success in your consulting engagements. By understanding and applying these key concepts, techniques, and tools, consultants can effectively navigate and manage conflicts, promoting collaboration, understanding, and successful resolution in their consulting engagements.

Practical Examples

Let's put that into practices.

Example 1: Resolving Team Conflict

During a consulting project for a manufacturing company, I encountered a significant conflict within the cross-functional team I was working with. The conflict arose due to differing opinions on the implementation of a new production process. The engineering team believed their approach was the most efficient, while the operations team had concerns about the potential impact on production timelines.

To address this conflict, I employed the Thomas-Kilmann Conflict Mode Instrument framework. I facilitated a meeting where each team member had the opportunity to express their concerns and perspectives. By actively listening and paraphrasing, I ensured that everyone felt heard and understood.

Next, I used a decision-making matrix to objectively evaluate the different options. The matrix considered factors such as feasibility, impact on production, and alignment with the company's strategic objectives. By involving the team in the decision-making process and considering their input, we reached a consensus on a modified approach that addressed the concerns of both teams.

Through effective communication and negotiation, we were able to resolve the conflict and implement the new production process successfully. The experience taught me the importance of understanding different perspectives, facilitating open dialogue, and utilizing conflict management tools to reach mutually beneficial outcomes.

Example 2: Client-Stakeholder Conflict

During another consulting engagement, I encountered a conflict between my client, a technology company, and one of their key stakeholders, a regulatory agency. The stakeholder had concerns about the potential environmental impact of the client's product, which created tension and threatened the project's progress.

To address this conflict, I utilized a combination of facilitation techniques and emotional intelligence. I scheduled a meeting with the stakeholder to understand their concerns and perspectives. Through active listening and empathy, I acknowledged their concerns and communicated the client's commitment to environmental sustainability.

During subsequent meetings, I employed facilitation techniques such as brainstorming and consensus-building to identify potential solutions. By creating a collaborative environment, I encouraged the client and stakeholder to explore mutually beneficial alternatives. Through constructive dialogue, we developed a revised product design that met the regulatory requirements while aligning with the client's business goals.

Throughout this process, emotional intelligence played a crucial role. I remained calm and composed, even during challenging conversations. By regulating my emotions and practicing assertiveness, I helped diffuse tension and build trust between the client and the stakeholder.

The successful resolution of this conflict strengthened the relationship between the client and the stakeholder, ensuring continued collaboration and a positive project outcome. This experience reinforced the significance of emotional intelligence, effective facilitation, and the power of collaboration in conflict resolution.

These examples illustrate how conflict resolution and management skills are vital for consultants. By employing appropriate conflict management tools, facilitating open dialogue, and leveraging emotional intelligence, consultants can navigate conflicts and achieve successful outcomes in their consulting engagements.

Challenges and Common Mistakes to Avoid

While conflict resolution is essential, there are also challenges and common mistakes to be aware of and avoid. In this sub-chapter, we'll explore potential pitfalls that consultants may face when managing conflicts. We'll discuss challenges such as dealing with emotions, maintaining impartiality, and managing power dynamics. We'll also highlight common mistakes to avoid, such as avoiding conflicts altogether, escalating conflicts unnecessarily, or using coercive tactics. By understanding these challenges and pitfalls, you can develop strategies to navigate conflicts more effectively and create win-win solutions.

Imagine yourself in the role of a consultant, facing a complex project with multiple stakeholders, competing interests, and inevitable conflicts along the way. As I, Cai Everdeen, share my personal experiences and reflections, we will explore the common challenges and mistakes to avoid when it comes to conflict resolution and management in the world of consulting.

Challenge 1: Avoiding or Ignoring Conflict - The Perils of Silence:

Picture a situation where tensions arise between team members, and rather than addressing them head-on, I chose to ignore them, hoping they would resolve themselves. This mistake only led to the conflict festering and becoming more difficult to manage. As a consultant, I have learned the importance of addressing conflicts proactively and creating a safe space for open dialogue.

Challenge 2: Lack of Effective Communication - The Power of Listening:

Recall a time when miscommunication exacerbated an already tense situation. In my journey as a consultant, I discovered the significance of effective communication and active listening. By listening attentively to all parties involved and fostering open and honest communication, I created an environment where conflicts could be resolved more constructively.

Challenge 3: Taking Sides - The Art of Neutrality:

Reflect on a scenario where you witnessed a consultant taking sides during a conflict. I have come to understand that taking sides compromises objectivity and hinders the ability to facilitate a fair resolution. As a consultant, my role is to remain neutral and guide the process of understanding different perspectives, encouraging collaboration, and finding common ground.

Challenge 4: Not Addressing Underlying Issues - Unveiling the Root Causes:

Consider a situation where conflicts repeatedly arose, seemingly out of nowhere. It became evident that surface-level conflicts were symptoms of deeper underlying issues. As a consultant, I have learned the importance of addressing these root causes by asking probing questions, fostering open dialogue, and uncovering the hidden dynamics at play.

Challenge 5: Lack of Emotional Intelligence - The Power of Empathy:

Recall a time when emotions ran high during a conflict resolution session. Emotional intelligence plays a crucial role in managing conflicts effectively. I discovered the significance of regulating emotions, empathizing with others, and approaching conflicts with a calm and empathetic demeanor. This enabled me to navigate difficult conversations and find mutually agreeable solutions.

Challenge 6: Insufficient Planning and Preparation - The Importance of Strategy:

Imagine entering a conflict resolution process without proper planning and preparation. This lack of strategy often leads to ineffective outcomes. As a consultant, I have learned the value of investing time in understanding the conflict, gathering relevant information, and developing a structured approach. This includes identifying stakeholders, setting clear objectives, and selecting appropriate conflict resolution techniques.

Challenge 7: Lack of Follow-up and Evaluation - Sustaining Resolution Outcomes:

Consider a situation where conflicts were resolved, but the agreements made were not implemented, leading to recurring issues. I realized the importance of follow-up and evaluation. As a consultant, I ensure that resolutions are put into action and periodically assess their effectiveness. This allows for necessary adjustments and promotes sustainable resolutions.

Throughout my journey as a consultant, I have encountered and learned from various challenges and mistakes in conflict resolution and management. By addressing conflicts proactively, fostering effective communication, maintaining neutrality, unveiling root causes, leveraging emotional intelligence, strategic planning, and sustaining resolution outcomes, consultants can navigate conflicts successfully and contribute to positive project outcomes and client relationships.

Remember, conflict is not something to be feared but an opportunity for growth and transformation. Embrace the challenges, learn from the mistakes, and master the art of conflict resolution as a consultant. By being aware of these challenges and avoiding these common mistakes, consultants can navigate conflicts more effectively and facilitate successful resolutions in their consulting engagements.

Exercises and Activities for Applying the Concepts

Through role-playing exercises, group discussions, and reflection, you'll enhance your ability to analyze conflicts, identify underlying interests, and generate creative solutions. And so, let's play!

Exercise 1: Role-Playing Scenarios

Create simulated conflict scenarios relevant to consulting situations. Divide participants into pairs or small groups, assigning each person a specific role. Ask them to engage in a role-play exercise where they have to resolve the conflict using the techniques discussed in the chapter. Afterward, facilitate a debriefing session to discuss the approaches used, strengths, areas for improvement, and lessons learned.

Exercise 2: Reflective Case Study Analysis

Provide case studies or real-life examples of conflicts that consultants commonly encounter. Ask readers to analyze the situations, identify the underlying issues, and propose conflict resolution strategies based on the concepts discussed. Encourage readers to reflect on their own experiences and draw parallels between the case studies and their own consulting practice.

Exercise 3: Conflict Mapping and Resolution Plan

Guide readers to select a recent or ongoing conflict they are experiencing in their consulting work. Ask them to create a conflict map, visually representing the key stakeholders, their interests, and the underlying causes of the conflict. Then, have them develop a comprehensive conflict resolution plan, considering the techniques and tools explored in the chapter. Encourage readers to implement the plan and reflect on its effectiveness in resolving the conflict.

These exercises provide opportunities for readers to practice applying conflict resolution and management techniques in a safe and structured environment. By engaging in these activities, readers can enhance their understanding and skills, ultimately improving their ability to navigate conflicts effectively in their consulting daily practice.

Conclusion

"Conflict is an opportunity for growth and innovation. By embracing and managing conflicts effectively, consultants can unlock new possibilities and achieve greater success for their clients."
– Unknown

In conclusion, the chapter on conflict resolution and management has provided valuable insights and strategies for effectively navigating conflicts in the consulting world. Here are the key points discussed:

Understanding Conflict: Conflict is an inevitable part of professional life, and consultants often encounter it in their work. It can arise from differences in opinions, priorities, or approaches, but it also presents opportunities for growth and innovation.

Approaches to Conflict Resolution: The chapter explored different approaches to conflict resolution, including collaboration, compromise, accommodation, avoidance, and competition. Each approach has its own advantages and considerations, and choosing the most appropriate approach depends on the situation and desired outcomes.

Effective Communication: Effective communication is crucial for resolving conflicts. The chapter emphasized the importance of active listening, clear and assertive communication, and empathy in understanding the perspectives and needs of others.

Conflict Resolution Strategies: The chapter introduced various strategies and techniques for managing conflicts, such as seeking common ground, reframing the issue, brainstorming solutions, and engaging in constructive dialogue. It also highlighted the importance of maintaining professionalism and focusing on finding win-win solutions.

Challenges and Mistakes to Avoid: The chapter discussed common challenges and mistakes in conflict resolution, such as escalating conflicts, taking things personally, and avoiding difficult conversations. It emphasized the need for self-awareness, emotional intelligence, and a proactive approach to addressing conflicts.

Developing Conflict Resolution Skills: The chapter suggested practical exercises and activities to develop conflict resolution skills, such as role-playing scenarios, practicing active listening, and seeking feedback from colleagues. These activities help consultants build their confidence and competence in managing conflicts.

Navigating conflicts effectively is a valuable skill for consultants, as it promotes collaboration, strengthens relationships, and enhances problem-solving abilities. By applying the strategies and techniques discussed in this chapter, consultants can transform conflicts into opportunities for growth and create positive outcomes for themselves and their clients. In the next chapter, we will explore the topic of Cross-Cultural Communication, where we will delve into the importance of understanding and navigating cultural differences in a global consulting context. Sounds like a plan?

Chapter 16: Cross-Cultural Communication

As I stepped off the plane onto foreign soil, I was filled with a mix of excitement and apprehension. I was about to embark on a consulting project in a new country, immersing myself in a culture vastly different from my own. Little did I know that this experience would not only test my consulting skills but also challenge my ability to communicate effectively across cultures.

Cross-cultural communication is an essential skill for consultants working in a globalized world. It refers to the ability to convey messages, ideas, and information between people from different cultural backgrounds in a way that is mutually understandable and respectful. It goes beyond language proficiency and encompasses understanding cultural norms, values, and communication styles.

Let's therefor explore the intricacies of cross-cultural communication and its significance in the consulting practice. In this chapter, we will delve into the key challenges and benefits of navigating diverse cultural contexts, and provide practical insights and tools to enhance your cross-cultural communication skills.

By developing a strong foundation in cross-cultural communication, you will be equipped to build rapport, establish trust, and effectively collaborate with clients and stakeholders from different cultural backgrounds. Let's embark on this journey together as we uncover the secrets to successful cross-cultural communication in the consulting world.

Introduction to the Cross-Cultural Communication

Welcome to the world of cross-cultural communication! In this chapter, we will explore the significance of effective communication in a diverse and multicultural consulting environment. Cross-cultural communication refers to the exchange of information, ideas, and messages between individuals from different cultural backgrounds. It involves understanding and adapting to the cultural nuances, values, and communication styles of others to ensure effective and meaningful communication.

As consultants, we often work with clients and colleagues from different cultural backgrounds, and understanding how to navigate and bridge cultural differences is crucial for building rapport, fostering collaboration, and achieving successful outcomes. In this sub-chapter, we will delve into the importance of cross-cultural communication and the impact it can have on consulting engagements.

For consultants, cross-cultural communication is of utmost importance due to the increasingly global nature of their work. Consultants often work with diverse clients and stakeholders from different cultural backgrounds. Being able to navigate and communicate effectively across cultures allows consultants to build trust, establish rapport, and form strong relationships with clients, ultimately leading to successful outcomes.

In the daily life of a consultant, cross-cultural communication means being aware of and respecting cultural differences in communication styles, body language, and business etiquette. It requires adapting one's communication approach to suit the cultural context and being mindful of potential cultural barriers or misunderstandings. It also involves actively listening, asking clarifying questions, and seeking to understand the perspectives and needs of individuals from different cultures. By mastering cross-cultural communication, consultants can bridge cultural divides, foster collaboration, and achieve better results in their consulting engagements.

Key Concepts, Techniques, and Tools

Once upon a time, in my early years as a consultant, I found myself embarking on a new project in a foreign country. Excitement and anticipation filled the air as I prepared to dive into a cross-cultural adventure. Little did I know, the journey would be both eye-opening and challenging, as I soon discovered the importance of cross-cultural communication in the world of consulting.

As I delved into this new venture, I realized that cross-cultural communication was not simply about speaking a different language or understanding customs; it was about embracing a whole new way of connecting with people from diverse backgrounds. Here are the key concepts, techniques, and tools that helped me navigate this cultural kaleidoscope:

Concept 1: Cultural Awareness

I recognized the need to immerse myself in the local culture, to understand its nuances, values, and beliefs. By doing so, I was able to appreciate the perspectives and expectations of my clients and build a foundation of trust and respect.

Cultural Awareness is a fundamental concept in the field of cross-cultural communication. It refers to having an understanding and appreciation of different cultural norms, values, beliefs, and practices. As a consultant, developing cultural awareness is essential for successfully navigating cross-cultural interactions and getting the most out of these experiences.

Here's how you can enhance your cultural awareness:

Embrace Curiosity: Approach each cultural encounter with a curious mindset. Be open to learning about different cultures and their unique characteristics. Ask questions, seek information, and strive to understand the underlying reasons behind cultural practices. Curiosity will fuel your desire to explore and appreciate cultural diversity.

Educate Yourself: Take the initiative to educate yourself about different cultures. Read books, articles, and blogs about the countries and communities you will be working with. Familiarize yourself with their history, customs, traditions, and social norms. This knowledge will serve as a foundation for understanding cultural nuances and avoiding misunderstandings.

Engage in Intercultural Experiences: Actively seek out opportunities to immerse yourself in different cultures. Travel to different countries, participate in cultural events, and engage with people from diverse backgrounds. This firsthand experience will provide valuable insights into different ways of thinking, behaving, and communicating.

Develop Empathy: Cultivate empathy by putting yourself in the shoes of individuals from other cultures. Try to understand their perspectives, values, and beliefs, and how these shape their behaviors and communication styles. Developing empathy will allow you to approach cross-cultural interactions with sensitivity and respect.

Build Relationships: Establish meaningful connections with individuals from different cultures. Actively listen to their stories, experiences, and perspectives. Building relationships based on trust and respect will create a safe space for open communication and exchange of ideas.

Reflect on Your Own Culture: Take the time to reflect on your own cultural background and how it influences your perceptions and behaviors. Recognize that your own cultural lens may shape your assumptions and biases. By becoming aware of your own cultural biases, you can better navigate cross-cultural situations and avoid making assumptions or judgments.

Seek Feedback: Be open to receiving feedback from individuals of different cultural backgrounds. Ask for their perspective on your communication style and behaviors. Their insights can help you gain a better understanding of how you are perceived and how you can adjust your approach to be more culturally sensitive.

By developing cultural awareness, you will be better equipped to adapt your communication style, build relationships, and navigate cross-cultural challenges in your consulting practice. It will enable you to work effectively with clients from diverse cultural backgrounds, foster mutual understanding, and create successful outcomes.

Concept 2: Verbal and Nonverbal Communication

I quickly realized that words were just one part of the equation. Nonverbal cues played a crucial role in conveying messages and establishing rapport. I learned to pay attention to body language, facial expressions, and tone of voice, adapting my own communication style to suit the cultural context.

Verbal and nonverbal communication play a crucial role in cross-cultural communication. Verbal communication refers to the use of words and language to convey messages, while nonverbal communication encompasses facial expressions, body language, gestures, and tone of voice. Mastering both forms of communication is essential for consultants to effectively navigate cross-cultural interactions. Here's how you can get the most out of verbal and nonverbal communication:

Verbal Communication

Language Proficiency: Develop proficiency in the language spoken by your clients or stakeholders. This will enable you to communicate directly without relying solely on interpreters or translators.

Clear and Simple Language: Use clear and simple language, avoiding complex jargon or idiomatic expressions that may not be easily understood by individuals from different cultural backgrounds.

Active Listening: Practice active listening by paying attention to what is being said, asking clarifying questions, and demonstrating genuine interest in understanding the perspectives and ideas being shared.

Adapt Communication Style: Adapt your communication style to suit the cultural context. Be mindful of the level of formality, directness, and politeness expected in different cultures.

Avoid Assumptions: Do not assume that certain words or phrases have the same meaning in all cultures. Be open to asking for clarification and ensuring mutual understanding.

Nonverbal Communication

Body Language Awareness: Familiarize yourself with common nonverbal cues and gestures in different cultures. Be aware that certain gestures or expressions may have different meanings or connotations in various cultural contexts.

Facial Expressions: Pay attention to facial expressions, as they can convey emotions and attitudes. Be mindful of cultural differences in interpreting and expressing emotions through facial expressions.

Eye Contact: Understand the cultural norms around eye contact. In some cultures, direct eye contact is a sign of respect and engagement, while in others, it may be considered rude or confrontational.

Gestures and Posture: Be cautious when using gestures, as they can have different meanings across cultures. Similarly, be aware of your posture, as it can convey openness or defensiveness.

Tone of Voice: Pay attention to your tone of voice, as it can influence how your message is perceived. Be mindful of cultural differences in vocal volume, pitch, and rhythm.

To get the most out of verbal and nonverbal communication in cross-cultural settings, it is crucial to practice cultural sensitivity, adaptability, and active observation. Developing cultural intelligence and seeking feedback from colleagues or mentors from different cultural backgrounds can further enhance your communication skills. Remember, effective cross-cultural communication is about building bridges of understanding and establishing meaningful connections with individuals from diverse cultures.

Concept 3: Active Listening

It became clear that active listening was key to bridging cultural gaps. I made a conscious effort to listen attentively, ask clarifying questions, and reflect back to ensure mutual understanding. This helped me avoid misunderstandings and establish stronger connections.

Active Listening in cross-cultural communication is the practice of fully engaging and understanding the speaker's message while being aware of cultural nuances and differences. It involves not only hearing the words being said but also paying attention to nonverbal cues, emotions, and underlying meanings. As a consultant, getting the most out of active listening can greatly enhance cross-cultural communication effectiveness. Here's how:

Be Present: Give your full attention to the speaker and avoid distractions. Show genuine interest and create a comfortable environment that encourages open communication.

Suspend Judgment: Put aside preconceived notions or stereotypes about the speaker's culture. Approach the conversation with an open mind and a willingness to learn and understand their perspective.

Listen to Understand: Focus on comprehending the speaker's message rather than formulating your response. Avoid interrupting or interjecting with your own thoughts or assumptions. Seek clarification if needed.

Pay Attention to Nonverbal Cues: Cultural differences may manifest through nonverbal cues such as body language, facial expressions, and tone of voice. Be observant and consider these cues in understanding the speaker's intended meaning.

Reflect and Paraphrase: Summarize and repeat what the speaker has said in your own words to ensure accurate understanding. This demonstrates that you are actively listening and encourages the speaker to provide further clarification if necessary.

Practice Empathy: Put yourself in the speaker's shoes and try to understand their emotions, motivations, and cultural background. This empathetic approach fosters connection and builds trust.

Be Patient: Cross-cultural communication may require additional time for information processing and response. Allow for pauses and silence, as it may indicate that the speaker is considering their words or cultural norms are at play.

Seek Feedback: After listening, confirm your understanding by asking clarifying questions or restating key points. This demonstrates your commitment to accurate comprehension and allows for course correction if needed.

Adapt your Communication Style: Recognize that your own communication style may need to be adjusted to accommodate cultural differences. Be mindful of language, tone, and level of formality to ensure effective communication.

By actively listening in cross-cultural communication, you can build stronger relationships, mitigate misunderstandings, and promote collaboration. It enables you to navigate cultural differences with sensitivity and respect, ultimately enhancing your effectiveness as a consultant in a global context.

Concept 4: Empathy and Respect

I understood that empathy and respect were vital in fostering positive relationships. I embraced the diversity of perspectives and customs, valuing the richness that each culture brought to the table. This created a safe space for open dialogue and collaboration.

Empathy and respect are foundational elements in the field of cross-cultural communication. They play a critical role in fostering understanding, building relationships, and navigating cultural differences. As a consultant, embracing empathy and respect in cross-cultural communication can greatly enhance your effectiveness. Here's what it means and how to get the most out of it:

Empathy: Empathy is the ability to understand and share the feelings, thoughts, and experiences of others. In cross-cultural communication, empathy involves putting yourself in the shoes of individuals from different cultural backgrounds, seeking to understand their perspectives and emotions. To cultivate empathy as a consultant:

- Listen actively and attentively to the concerns, needs, and ideas of others.
- Practice perspective-taking by imagining yourself in their cultural context.
- Show genuine interest and curiosity in learning about their cultural values, beliefs, and practices.
- Validate their experiences and emotions without judgment or bias.
- Demonstrate empathy through verbal and nonverbal cues, such as nodding, maintaining eye contact, and using reflective statements.

Respect: Respect involves recognizing and valuing the worth, dignity, and diversity of individuals and their cultural backgrounds. In cross-cultural communication, respect means honoring and appreciating the unique perspectives and customs of others. To demonstrate respect as a consultant:

- Approach interactions with an open mind and a willingness to learn.
- Avoid making assumptions or generalizations about people based on their culture.
- Engage in active listening and show genuine interest in understanding their cultural practices and values.
- Use inclusive language and avoid using stereotypes or derogatory terms.
- Adapt your communication style to align with cultural norms and customs, demonstrating sensitivity and flexibility.

By embracing empathy and respect in your cross-cultural communication, you can create an inclusive and collaborative environment that fosters trust and understanding. This, in turn, enables you to build stronger relationships with clients, effectively navigate cultural differences, and achieve successful outcomes in your consulting engagements. Remember, empathy and respect are ongoing practices that require continuous self-reflection and a commitment to cultural competence.

Concept 5: Adaptability

I learned to be adaptable and flexible in my communication approach. I adjusted my language, level of formality, and even my sense of humor to align with the cultural norms of my clients. This willingness to adapt made a significant difference in building connections and breaking down barriers.

Adaptability in cross-cultural communication refers to the ability to adjust and modify one's behavior, communication style, and mindset to effectively interact with individuals from different cultural backgrounds. As a consultant, being adaptable in cross-cultural communication is essential for building rapport, understanding diverse perspectives, and successfully navigating intercultural interactions. Here's how you can get the most out of adaptability in the cross-cultural communication field:

Embrace Cultural Differences: Approach each cross-cultural encounter with an open mind and a willingness to embrace cultural differences. Recognize that there is no universal "right" or "wrong" way of doing things, and that cultural norms and practices can vary greatly. Seek to understand and appreciate the cultural context of your clients or colleagues.

Learn and Observe: Take the time to educate yourself about the cultural values, customs, and communication styles of the people you are working with. Learn about their history, traditions, and social norms. Observe how people communicate and interact in different cultural settings, and adapt your own behavior accordingly.

Flexibility in Communication: Be flexible in your communication style. Adjust your language, tone, and level of formality to align with the cultural norms of your audience. Pay attention to nonverbal cues and adapt your body language and gestures to convey respect and understanding. Use appropriate greetings, honorifics, and other cultural communication norms.

Be a Perceptive Listener: Actively listen and observe during cross-cultural interactions. Be attentive to verbal and nonverbal cues, as well as the underlying meaning behind words. Practice empathy and seek to understand the perspectives and emotions of others. Avoid making assumptions or imposing your own cultural biases.

Seek Feedback: Be open to receiving feedback from individuals from different cultural backgrounds. Ask for their perspective on your communication style and effectiveness. Their insights can help you identify areas for improvement and further refine your adaptability in cross-cultural communication.

Cultivate Cultural Intelligence (CQ): Cultivate your cultural intelligence, which refers to your ability to navigate and work effectively in diverse cultural contexts. Continuously educate yourself about different cultures, their values, and communication styles. Develop your intercultural sensitivity and competence through training programs, workshops, and intercultural experiences.

Emphasize Common Ground: Focus on finding common ground and shared goals with individuals from different cultures. Identify shared values, interests, or objectives that can serve as a foundation for collaboration and understanding. Building relationships based on commonalities can help bridge cultural gaps and foster effective communication.

By embracing adaptability in cross-cultural communication, you can enhance your effectiveness as a consultant in multicultural settings. It allows you to connect with clients, build trust, and navigate potential cultural challenges with grace and understanding.

Concept 6: Conflict Resolution

I discovered that conflicts could arise due to cultural differences, and I needed to be equipped with effective conflict resolution skills. Active listening, finding common ground, and seeking win-win solutions became essential tools in navigating cross-cultural conflicts and maintaining positive working relationships.

Conflict resolution in the cross-cultural communication field refers to the process of addressing and resolving conflicts that arise due to cultural differences. As a consultant, mastering conflict resolution in cross-cultural contexts is essential for effective communication and successful collaborations. Here's how you can get the most out of it:

Cultural Sensitivity: Develop cultural sensitivity by understanding and respecting different cultural perspectives, values, and communication styles. Recognize that conflicts may arise from cultural misunderstandings, and approach them with empathy and respect.

Active Listening: Practice active listening to truly understand the concerns and viewpoints of all parties involved in the conflict. Listen attentively, ask clarifying questions, and paraphrase to ensure accurate understanding.

Perspective-taking: Put yourself in the shoes of others and try to see the situation from their cultural lens. This helps in understanding their motivations, needs, and concerns, and facilitates finding common ground.

Communication Clarity: Communicate clearly and explicitly, using simple and concise language, especially when there are language barriers. Avoid assumptions and provide detailed explanations to ensure understanding.

Mediation Skills: Develop mediation skills to facilitate productive discussions and find mutually acceptable solutions. Act as a neutral third party, guiding the conversation, and fostering a cooperative atmosphere.

Adaptability: Be adaptable and flexible in your conflict resolution approach, considering the cultural context and preferences of the parties involved. Adjust your communication style, negotiation strategies, and conflict resolution techniques to align with cultural norms.

Cultural Mediators: Seek the assistance of cultural mediators or intercultural specialists who can provide insights and help navigate the cultural nuances of the conflict. Their expertise can facilitate understanding and bridge gaps between different cultural perspectives.

Conflict Prevention: Focus on proactive conflict prevention by fostering open communication, setting clear expectations, and promoting a culture of respect and understanding. Address potential conflicts early on to prevent escalation.

Continuous Learning: Embrace a growth mindset and continuously expand your knowledge and understanding of different cultures. Attend cultural competency training programs, read books, and engage in intercultural experiences to enhance your conflict resolution skills.

By applying these strategies, consultants can effectively navigate conflicts arising from cultural differences, foster productive relationships, and create a harmonious working environment. Conflict resolution in cross-cultural communication is an opportunity for learning and growth, enabling consultants to build stronger connections and achieve successful outcomes.

Concept 7: Intercultural Communication Training

Recognizing the need to continuously develop my cross-cultural communication skills, I actively sought out training programs and workshops. These experiences provided valuable insights into specific cultural dimensions and helped me improve my intercultural understanding and competence.

Intercultural Communication Training is a specialized program or workshop designed to enhance an individual's ability to effectively communicate and collaborate across different cultures. As a consultant, it is crucial to invest in and leverage this training to get the most out of your cross-cultural interactions. Here's how you can make the most of it:

Seek Out Training Opportunities: Actively look for intercultural communication training programs or workshops that align with your specific needs and goals. Research reputable organizations or trainers who specialize in this field. Online courses, seminars, and in-person training sessions are all valuable options to consider.

Embrace a Learning Mindset: Approach the training with an open and curious mindset. Recognize that cultural differences can have a profound impact on communication and collaboration. Be willing to challenge your assumptions, learn about different cultural norms, and expand your cultural knowledge.

Participate Actively: Engage fully in the training sessions. Take part in discussions, ask questions, and share your experiences. Actively participate in activities and exercises that simulate cross-cultural scenarios to gain practical insights into effective communication strategies.

Develop Cultural Self-Awareness: Intercultural communication training often starts with developing self-awareness about your own cultural biases, assumptions, and communication patterns. Reflect on your own cultural background, values, and communication style. This awareness will help you understand how your cultural lens may influence your interactions with others.

Learn about Different Cultural Dimensions: Explore various cultural dimensions, such as communication styles, hierarchy, decision-making processes, and time orientation. Understanding these differences will enable you to adapt your communication approach and avoid misunderstandings.

Build Cross-Cultural Communication Skills: Intercultural communication training equips you with practical skills for effective communication across cultures. These skills may include active listening, empathy, adapting verbal and nonverbal communication, and conflict resolution techniques specific to cross-cultural contexts. Practice these skills during the training and apply them in real-life scenarios.

Foster Intercultural Competence: Intercultural competence is the ability to navigate and adapt to diverse cultural contexts. Develop your intercultural competence by embracing diversity, being open to new perspectives, and cultivating empathy and respect for different cultures. This competence will enable you to build strong relationships and collaborate effectively with clients from diverse backgrounds.

Apply the Learning: After the training, make a conscious effort to apply what you have learned in your consulting practice. Seek opportunities to engage with clients from different cultural backgrounds and practice your newly acquired skills. Reflect on your experiences, identify areas for improvement, and continue to develop your intercultural communication competence.

By actively engaging in intercultural communication training and applying the knowledge and skills gained, you will enhance your ability to navigate the complexities of cross-cultural interactions as a consultant. This will not only strengthen your relationships with clients but also contribute to the success of your consulting engagements in an increasingly globalized world.

Concept 8: Cultural Intelligence (CQ)

I realized that cultural intelligence, the ability to adapt and work effectively across cultures, was a crucial asset. I cultivated my CQ by staying open-minded, curious, and willing to learn from others' cultural perspectives. This mindset allowed me to approach each cross-cultural interaction with curiosity and humility.

Cultural Intelligence (CQ) is the ability to effectively and appropriately interact and work with people from different cultural backgrounds. It goes beyond simply recognizing and understanding cultural differences; it involves adapting and adjusting one's behavior to be more culturally sensitive and responsive.

As a consultant, developing and harnessing Cultural Intelligence can greatly enhance your cross-cultural communication skills and effectiveness. Here's how you can get the most out of it:

Develop Cultural Knowledge: Invest time in learning about different cultures, their customs, values, beliefs, and communication styles. Read books, engage in cultural immersion experiences, and seek out resources that can deepen your understanding of diverse cultural perspectives.

Embrace Curiosity and Open-mindedness: Approach cross-cultural interactions with a genuine curiosity and a willingness to learn from others. Be open-minded and avoid making assumptions or generalizations based on stereotypes. Instead, seek to understand the unique experiences and perspectives of individuals from different cultures.

Practice Empathy and Respect: Cultivate empathy by putting yourself in the shoes of others and striving to understand their cultural context. Show respect for diverse viewpoints and honor the values and customs of different cultures. This mindset will create a foundation of trust and mutual respect in your interactions.

Adapt Communication Styles: Recognize that communication styles vary across cultures. Adapt your communication approach by being aware of language barriers, adjusting your tone and body language, and using culturally appropriate expressions. Flexibility and adaptability in your communication style will help bridge cultural gaps.

Seek Feedback and Reflect: Actively seek feedback from colleagues, clients, and individuals from different cultures. Reflect on your own behaviors and interactions, and be open to constructive criticism. This feedback will help you identify areas for improvement and further develop your Cultural Intelligence.

Build Relationships and Networks: Engage in meaningful relationships with individuals from different cultural backgrounds. Seek opportunities to collaborate, learn from each other, and build networks of diverse professionals. This will broaden your cultural perspectives and provide valuable insights for your consulting work.

Embrace Continuous Learning: Cross-cultural communication is a lifelong learning process. Stay curious and continue to expand your knowledge and understanding of different cultures. Seek out professional development opportunities, such as workshops, courses, or intercultural training programs, to further enhance your Cultural Intelligence.

By developing and leveraging your Cultural Intelligence, you can navigate the complexities of cross-cultural communication with confidence and effectiveness. It allows you to build stronger relationships, better understand the needs and expectations of clients from diverse backgrounds, and ultimately excel in your role as a consultant in a globalized world.

As my journey unfolded, I learned that cross-cultural communication was not just a skill to acquire, but a lifelong adventure of exploration and growth. It opened doors to new perspectives, expanded my cultural horizons, and enriched my consulting practice. By embracing the key concepts, techniques, and tools of cross-cultural communication, I was able to navigate the cultural kaleidoscope and create meaningful connections with clients from around the world.

By incorporating these key concepts, techniques, and tools into their communication practices, consultants can navigate cross-cultural challenges more effectively and establish successful relationships with clients and stakeholders from different cultural backgrounds.

Practical Examples

Here are a couple of practical examples that illustrate the importance of cross-cultural communication in the world of consulting:

Example 1: Working with a Multicultural Team

A friend of mine, Marko, was assigned to a consulting project that involved a multicultural team consisting of individuals from different countries and cultural backgrounds. During the initial team meeting, Marko noticed that there were differences in communication styles and decision-making approaches. Some team members were more direct and assertive, while others were more reserved and preferred a consensus-based approach.

To navigate this cross-cultural dynamic, Marko realized the importance of adapting their communication style. They encouraged open and inclusive discussions, actively sought input from all team members, and facilitated a collaborative decision-making process. By acknowledging and respecting the diverse perspectives within the team, Marko fostered an inclusive environment that led to more effective collaboration and a successful project outcome.

Example 2: Client Engagement in a Foreign Country

I was assigned to work on a consulting project for a client based in a foreign country with a different cultural context. As a digital nomad, recognizing the significance of cross-cultural communication, I took the time to research and understand the local customs, business etiquette, and communication norms in that country. I wanted to work there and spend a few months visiting. A win-win; Anyway!

During client meetings, I adapted my communication style by using appropriate greetings, showing respect for hierarchical structures, and demonstrating cultural sensitivity. I also paid attention to non-verbal cues and used active listening techniques to ensure I understood the client's needs and expectations accurately.

By incorporating cross-cultural communication strategies, I managed to build trust and rapport with the client, which strengthened the consultant-client relationship. This enabled me to effectively navigate cultural differences, communicate complex ideas, and ultimately deliver a successful project outcome.

These two simple examples highlight the importance of cross-cultural communication in consulting. It is crucial for consultants to recognize and adapt to cultural differences, communicate effectively, and build strong relationships with clients and colleagues from diverse cultural backgrounds. By doing so, consultants can navigate cultural nuances, enhance collaboration, and achieve successful outcomes in their consulting projects.

Challenges and Common Mistakes to Avoid

As consultants, we often find ourselves working with clients from diverse cultural backgrounds. This brings both opportunities and challenges to our work. In this chapter, I will share with you some personal anecdotes and insights about the importance of cross-cultural communication and the common challenges and mistakes to avoid. By understanding these challenges and pitfalls, you can develop cultural intelligence and improve your ability to communicate effectively across cultures.

Challenge 1: Stereotyping and Generalizations

I vividly remember my first international consulting project where I was assigned to work with a team from a different cultural background. I had preconceived notions about their communication style based on stereotypes I had heard. However, I soon realized that each team member had their own unique way of expressing themselves. It was a valuable lesson that taught me to avoid making generalizations and approach each individual with an open mind.

Recognize that cultural norms and behaviors can vary widely, even within a single culture. Avoid assuming that everyone from a specific culture will have the same communication style or approach. Embrace diversity and be open to learning from different perspectives.

Challenge 2: Language and Communication Barriers

During a consulting engagement in a non-English speaking country, I faced significant language barriers. My attempts to communicate in the local language were met with confusion, and important details were getting lost in translation. I quickly realized the importance of finding common ground in communication. We started using visual aids, diagrams, and simplified language to ensure clarity and understanding.

Language differences can pose challenges in cross-cultural communication. It is crucial to address language barriers through effective communication strategies such as using clear and concise language, avoiding jargon or slang, and actively listening to understand and clarify any misunderstandings.

Challenge 3: Non-Verbal Communication

Once, during a meeting with a client from a different cultural background, I noticed that they seemed reserved and less expressive compared to what I was accustomed to. I later learned that the reserved demeanor was a cultural norm in their culture. By adapting my own non-verbal cues to match theirs and being mindful of their personal space, we were able to establish a more comfortable and productive working relationship.

Non-verbal cues and body language can vary across cultures and may be interpreted differently. Pay attention to cultural differences in gestures, eye contact, personal space, and other non-verbal communication cues. Adapting accordingly can help avoid misinterpretations and build rapport.

Challenge 4: Cultural Sensitivity and Respect

In a cross-cultural consulting project, I once unintentionally made a remark that was considered offensive in the client's culture. It caused tension and strained our working relationship. I quickly realized the importance of cultural sensitivity and the need to show respect for different cultural norms and customs. I apologized sincerely and took the time to learn more about their cultural values to avoid similar mistakes in the future.

Lack of cultural sensitivity and respect can hinder effective cross-cultural communication. Be aware of cultural norms, values, and customs, and show respect for them. Avoid making insensitive or offensive remarks, and demonstrate empathy and understanding towards different cultural perspectives.

Challenge 5: Lack of Awareness and Adaptability

In a recent project, I had the opportunity to work with a diverse team comprising individuals from various cultural backgrounds. Initially, I faced challenges in understanding and adapting to their communication styles. However, I took the initiative to learn more about their cultures, sought their feedback, and actively worked on adapting my own communication approach. This resulted in improved collaboration and strengthened our working relationships.

Lack of awareness and adaptability to different cultural contexts can hinder effective cross-cultural communication. Invest time in learning about the cultures you interact with, seek cultural training or coaching if necessary. Be open-minded, flexible, and willing to adapt communication styles and approaches to navigate cross-cultural challenges more effectively.

Cross-cultural communication is a vital skill for consultants working in today's globalized world. By avoiding common challenges and mistakes such as stereotyping, language barriers, non-verbal communication misunderstandings, lack of cultural sensitivity, and inflexibility, we can enhance our ability to communicate effectively across cultures. Embracing cultural diversity and being mindful of different communication styles will enable us to build stronger relationships, foster collaboration, and achieve successful outcomes in our consulting projects.

By being mindful of these challenges and avoiding common mistakes, consultants can enhance their cross-cultural communication skills and build stronger relationships with clients and colleagues from different cultural backgrounds. This will lead to more effective collaboration, better understanding, and successful outcomes in consulting projects.

Exercises and Activities for Applying the Concepts

The best exercise I'd recommend you is to travel! Travel the world! Explore! Learn from various cultures! But, let me be more practical here, today. Here are two exercises that can help readers apply the concepts of cross-cultural communication in their consulting daily practice:

Exercise 1: Cultural Immersion Project

Choose a culture that you frequently interact with or are interested in learning more about. Spend some time researching and immersing yourself in the customs, traditions, and communication styles of that culture. Try to understand their values, beliefs, and norms. Reflect on how this knowledge can impact your interactions and communication with individuals from that culture. This exercise will help you develop a deeper understanding and appreciation for different cultures and enhance your cross-cultural communication skills.

Exercise 2: Role-Play Scenarios

Create role-play scenarios that involve cross-cultural communication challenges. Assign different cultural backgrounds to participants and have them act out typical consulting situations. Encourage participants to use effective cross-cultural communication techniques such as active listening, clarifying understanding, and adapting communication styles. After each role-play, discuss the challenges encountered and explore strategies to overcome them. This exercise will allow you to practice and refine your cross-cultural communication skills in a safe and controlled environment.

Exercise 3: Cultural Exchange Lunches

Organize regular lunch or coffee sessions with colleagues or clients from different cultural backgrounds. Use these informal gatherings as an opportunity to engage in open discussions about cultural practices, communication styles, and any challenges faced in cross-cultural interactions. Share personal experiences and insights, and encourage others to do the same. This activity will promote cultural understanding, foster relationships, and provide a platform to learn from one another's experiences.

Remember, the key to these exercises is reflection and learning. Take time to reflect on the outcomes of each exercise and how you can apply the lessons learned in your consulting practice. By actively engaging in these activities, you will develop a greater sensitivity to cultural differences and improve your cross-cultural communication skills.

Conclusion

"Communication is the bridge that connects cultures and opens doors to mutual understanding and collaboration. By embracing and mastering cross-cultural communication, consultants can build bridges that lead to successful partnerships and global success." – Unknown

Here are the key points discussed:

Importance of Cross-Cultural Communication: In an interconnected and diverse world, cross-cultural communication is essential for successful consulting engagements. It involves understanding and adapting to different cultural norms, values, and communication styles to build effective relationships and avoid misunderstandings.

Cultural Intelligence: Developing cultural intelligence allows consultants to navigate diverse cultural contexts with sensitivity and respect. It includes being aware of one's own cultural biases, actively seeking knowledge about other cultures, and adapting communication and behavior accordingly.

Communication Styles and Strategies: The chapter introduced various communication styles and strategies, such as direct and indirect communication, high and low context communication, and nonverbal communication. It emphasized the importance of adapting communication styles to align with cultural norms and preferences.

Building Trust and Rapport: Trust and rapport are crucial in cross-cultural consulting. The chapter discussed the importance of building trust through active listening, demonstrating respect, and showing empathy towards different cultural perspectives.

Overcoming Cultural Barriers: Cultural barriers, such as language barriers, stereotypes, and assumptions, can hinder effective communication. The chapter highlighted the need to be mindful of these barriers and actively work to overcome them through open-mindedness, curiosity, and a willingness to learn.

Sensitivity to Cultural Differences: Sensitivity to cultural differences is essential for successful consulting engagements. The chapter emphasized the need to approach cultural differences with curiosity, respect, and an open mind. It also encouraged consultants to seek feedback and learn from their experiences.

In summary, cross-cultural communication and sensitivity are critical skills for consultants working in a global context. By developing cultural intelligence, understanding different communication styles, building trust, and being sensitive to cultural differences, consultants can effectively navigate diverse cultural contexts and build strong relationships with clients and colleagues.

Conclusion

In conclusion, Part 2 of "*Consulting 102: The Advanced Guide for Consultants*" has been a journey into the realm of advanced communication and interpersonal skills. We have explored various topics, each shedding light on different aspects of effective communication and relationship building in the consulting world.

Chapter 9 focused on advanced presentation skills, emphasizing the importance of structuring compelling presentations, using visual aids effectively, and engaging with the audience to deliver impactful messages.

Chapter 10 introduced advanced facilitation skills, highlighting the techniques for guiding group discussions, managing conflicts, and fostering collaboration to achieve desired outcomes in client interactions.

Chapter 11 delved into the realm of executive presence and influence, exploring how consultants can establish credibility, build trust, and effectively influence key stakeholders to drive decision-making and implementation.

Chapter 12 brought the power of storytelling to the forefront, illustrating how compelling narratives can captivate audiences, convey complex ideas, and evoke emotional connections, ultimately influencing the decision-making process.

Chapter 13 focused on advanced negotiation skills, providing insights into strategic negotiation techniques, effective communication, and creating win-win outcomes in high-stakes consulting engagements.

Chapter 14 delved into the realm of emotional intelligence, highlighting the importance of self-awareness, empathy, and emotional management in building strong relationships, understanding client needs, and navigating challenging situations with finesse.

Chapter 15 explored conflict resolution and management, equipping consultants with strategies to identify and address conflicts early on, foster productive dialogue, and turn conflicts into opportunities for growth and collaboration.

Chapter 16 addressed the crucial aspect of cross-cultural communication, emphasizing the need for cultural sensitivity, adaptability, and effective communication in multicultural and global consulting environments.

Each chapter in Part 2 has provided valuable insights and practical techniques to enhance your communication and interpersonal skills as a consultant. By mastering these skills, you can establish credibility, foster effective collaboration, and build strong relationships with clients and stakeholders.

Remember, effective communication is not only about conveying information but also about understanding and connecting with others. By honing these skills, you can elevate your consulting practice, deepen your impact, and create lasting relationships with your clients.

As we conclude Part 2, I encourage you to reflect on the key takeaways from each chapter and consider how you can apply these insights and techniques in your consulting engagements. By continually honing your communication and interpersonal skills, you will position yourself as a trusted advisor, an effective collaborator, and a valued partner to your clients.

So, what's next you may wonder... well, let me tell you:

Well, in Part 3, we'll into essential business knowledge, such as financial analysis, marketing strategies, organizational behavior, and data analysis. These chapters provided you with a deeper understanding of the business landscape, enabling you to provide insightful and impactful recommendations to your clients.

Finally, in Part 4, we'll explore advanced consulting business management topics, including sales and business development, team management, ethics and professional conduct, and legal issues. These chapters equipped you with the knowledge and strategies necessary to establish and grow a successful consulting practice.

As you know, and heard me saying a thousand-time, continuous learning, adaptability, and maintaining a client-centric focus are critical to become a master at consulting. And so, as consultants, our success is intertwined with the success of our clients. We must always strive to provide exceptional value and innovative solutions that drive their growth and success.

In the words of the renowned management consultant, Peter Drucker, *"The best way to predict the future is to create it."* As consultants, we have the privilege of shaping the future through our expertise, insights, and dedication to our clients' success. So let us embrace this ongoing journey of learning and improvement, always striving to create a better future for our clients and ourselves.

I hope this second book in the Consulting 102 series has provided you with the knowledge, inspiration, and confidence to excel in your consulting career. Remember, consulting is a never-ending journey of growth and learning. So, as you navigate the challenges and opportunities that come your way, may you always approach each engagement with an open mind, a passion for excellence, and a relentless pursuit of client success.

Thank you for joining me on this adventure, may your consulting journey be filled with purpose, impact, and continuous success, and I hope to talk to you soon, in my next module of this series!

Happy Consulting!

Cai Everdeen.

About the Author

Hello! I'm Cai Everdeen.

I have 20 years (plus) of experience in the technology and consulting industry. I began my career as a Software Engineer in Energy and Utilities. I then tried this Consulting *thing* for a few years. And, life being what it is, I then worked seven years as a Senior Staff Software Engineer at Tesla where I gained a wealth of experience in the field of advanced product development.

Since 2019, I've been exploring new opportunities and challenging myself in new ways. I indeed took the leap and became a digital nomad, a self-published author, while consulting for start-up businesses to Fortune 500 companies.

Also, By the Author

Financial Freedom: Practical Tips and Real-life Examples

The short book begins by defining financial freedom and explaining why it is important for individuals and families. From there, it goes on to cover key topics such as creating a budget, paying off debt, improving credit scores, saving and investing for the long term, increasing income, advancing careers, planning for financial goals, protecting assets, and planning for the future with insurance and estate planning.

Throughout the short book, you will find practical tips, real-life examples, and expert advice to help you achieve financial freedom and build a solid foundation for long-term financial stability. Whether you are just starting out on your financial journey or looking to take your financial planning to the next level, this short book has something for everyone. So, join us on this journey towards financial freedom and start making progress today!

As a digital nomad myself, I know firsthand the challenges and opportunities that come with the digital nomad lifestyle. I've faced many obstacles and learned many valuable lessons along the way, and I'm excited to share my experiences with you.

In this book, you'll learn about the pros and cons of the digital nomad lifestyle, the types of jobs and industries that lend themselves well to remote work, and how to build a diverse set of skills that can be easily transferred to a remote work environment. You'll also learn about the top 10 tips and challenges of the digital nomad lifestyle and the best countries for US citizens to consider moving to for beginning their journey as a digital nomad.

To be concise and to the point, this book is written as Frequently Asked Questions. By the end of this book, you'll have a better understanding of what it takes to make the switch to a digital nomad lifestyle, and you'll be equipped with the knowledge and resources you need to make it happen.

Welcome to Scientific Breakthroughs, Volume 1! This book delves into the top 25 scientific breakthroughs of the 1980s and 1990s that have changed the way we think about the world and have had a profound impact on our lives. This book is a journey through the scientific discoveries, highlighting how these breakthroughs have changed our lives for the better and exploring the ethical and societal implications that came along with them.

This book will take you through the scientific details of these breakthroughs and explore the ways in which they have changed our understanding of the world. You will learn about the scientific principles behind these discoveries and gain a deeper understanding of how they work. And along the way, we will also delve into the ethical and societal implications of these breakthroughs and discuss the ways in which they have changed the way we think about the world.

This book is not just for scientists and researchers, but also for anyone with an interest in the world around them. We hope that by reading this book, you will gain a new appreciation for the power of science to change our lives, and an understanding of the importance of considering the ethical and societal implications of scientific discoveries.

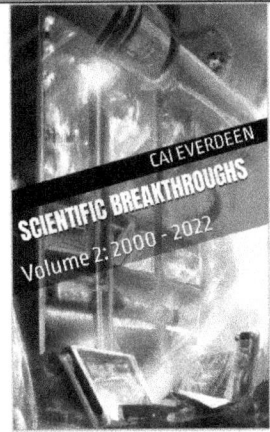

And here we are! It's sequel time! The Volume 2! Yes, indeed! And in this second book, we'll delve into the top 25+ scientific breakthroughs of the 2000s and 2010s.

In this second book, we'll tell you a story, we'll narrate a fantastic journey through the scientific discoveries of the past two decades, highlighting how these breakthroughs have changed our lives, and exploring the societal implications that came along with these breakthroughs.

This book will take you through the scientific details of these breakthroughs and explore the ways in which they have changed our understanding of the world. You will learn about the scientific principles behind these discoveries and gain a deeper understanding of how they work. And along the way, we will also delve into the ethical and societal implications of these breakthroughs and discuss the ways in which they have changed the way we think about the world.

Like the first volume, this book is not just for scientists and researchers. It's for anyone interesting in the world around them. If you're curious. If you like to read and learn. Well, we hope this second volume will allow you to gain a new appreciation for the power of science, and an understanding of the importance of considering the ethical implications of scientific discoveries.

We did it! We combined both Volume 1 and 2 of the Scientific Breakthroughs series into one book! And so, this book delves into the top 50 scientific breakthroughs from 1980 to 2022 that have changed the way we think about the world and have had a profound impact on our lives. This book is a journey through the scientific discoveries, highlighting how these breakthroughs have changed our lives for the better and exploring the ethical and societal implications that came along with them.

This book is not just for scientists and researchers, but also for anyone with an interest in the world around them. We hope that by reading this book, you will gain a new appreciation for the power of science to change our lives, and an understanding of the importance of considering the ethical and societal implications of scientific discoveries.

When I first became interested in artificial intelligence (AI) in the early 1990s, I was immediately struck by the incredible potential of this technology to change the world. From healthcare to retail, from customer service to automobiles, from finance to security, AI has the power to revolutionize virtually every industry and aspect of our lives.

But as I delved deeper into the field, I also realized that AI is not without its ethical and societal implications. As the technology has advanced, it has raised important questions about privacy, autonomy, bias, and accountability.

In this book, the Volume 3 in the Scientific Breakthroughs series, I aim to take you on a journey through the key scientific breakthroughs in AI over the last several decades. I'll dive into the history of AI, exploring the development of expert systems, artificial neural networks, fuzzy logic, natural language processing, computer vision, decision support systems, self-driving cars, speech recognition, virtual and augmented reality, and more.

But this book is not just about the technology itself. I'll also explore the ways in which these breakthroughs are being applied in various fields, from healthcare to retail, from customer service to automobiles, from finance to security.

As a consultant, you must possess a unique blend of technical knowledge, problem-solving skills, and soft skills.

In this book, I have combined my own experiences and insights to create a comprehensive guide to the essential soft skills in consulting. The book is organized into five chapters, each focusing on communication, problem-solving, teamwork, adaptability, and integrity.

Whether you're an aspiring consultant, a seasoned professional, or simply looking to develop your soft skills, this book is for you! In fact, I hope it will serve as a valuable resource to grow and succeed in your consulting career.

Consulting 101: The Two-Week Transition OR The Secrets to Ramp-Up Quickly

As a consultant, I understand the challenges of navigating new projects and delivering high-quality results within tight time frames. And so, in this follow-up book, I want to provide you with a step-by-step approach to effectively manage the first two weeks of a new consulting engagement.

The strategies, tools and techniques outlined in this book should help you prepare for the transition, build strong relationships with your clients, and deliver high-quality work that meets and exceeds their expectations.

Whether you are a seasoned consultant or just starting your consulting career, this book is packed with practical tips and advice that will help you succeed in your next consulting engagement!

In this book, we'll take a journey through the world of renewable energy and discover the latest breakthroughs in solar, wind, hydro, geothermal, and bio energy. We'll also explore the importance of energy storage and how it can help us unlock the full potential of these clean energy sources.

Whether you're a science enthusiast, a student, a policymaker, or simply a curious reader, this book is for you. It's a chance to discover the incredible potential of renewable energy and to explore the breakthroughs that are already making a difference in people's lives.

As someone who comes from a family with many ancestors who lived well into their centennial years, I've always been curious about what factors contribute to a long and healthy life. Over the years, I've read countless books, attended seminars, and interviewed experts in the field of aging and longevity. I've also experimented with different diets, exercise routines, and lifestyle habits to see what works best for me.

Through this book, I want to share with you what I've learned about healthy living and longevity. My goal is to provide you with practical, evidence-based recommendations that you can apply to your own life, regardless of your age or current health status.

The book is divided into eight chapters, each focusing on a different aspect of healthy living and longevity. From nutrition and exercise to sleep and stress management, you'll learn about the latest research and best practices for optimizing your health and wellbeing.

I hope this book will serve as a valuable resource and guide for anyone who wants to live a longer, healthier, and more fulfilling life. Whether you're in your 20s or your 80s, it's never too late to start making positive changes that can benefit your health and wellbeing for years to come.

In this comprehensive guide, you'll dive into agile consulting methodologies, design thinking, systems thinking, advanced strategic planning, innovation and creativity techniques, process improvement methodologies, project management and advanced change management practices.

With practical examples and exercises, this guide offers a hands-on approach to help you navigate the challenges and seize the opportunities that come with being a consultant.

This page intentionally left blank.

www.ingramcontent.com/pod-product-compliance
Lightning Source LLC
Chambersburg PA
CBHW060824220526
45466CB00003B/962

* 9 7 9 8 3 9 8 1 4 4 0 9 3 *